Benzo-Wise: A Recovery Companion

Everything you need to know to cope successfully with benzodiazepine withdrawal

"This is an inspirational book, very clearly written and easy to understand.... The author explains various coping mechanisms, takes a look at diet and supplements and confronts the issue of suicidal thoughts. There is also a chapter on how to support someone going through withdrawal, very useful for friends and family to read.... Tells you what you really need to know about coming off benzos."

~Martha Langley, co-author of *Free Yourself from Anxiety*

"I had many reactions after reading the book (all of them positive) but the biggest was a sense of gratitude that the author was sharing her story and in a sense validating what all of us in withdrawal are experiencing. The author's writing is gentle, reassuring and you feel as if you are not alone on this journey, but that she is there cheering you on. She covers all aspects of the recovery process from tapering to coping to visits with disbelieving doctors. The format of the book is sensitive to those coping with brain fog, comprehension problems and memory disruptions. During my difficult waves (especially the anxiety) her writing and coping suggestions have helped me tremendously. I would recommend this book highly to anyone going through any kind of withdrawal or chronic illness as well as anyone in the medical or mental health community as there is a section for doctors as well as counselors."

~Heather, benzo survivor, Northwest USA

"I'm late into my withdrawal but wish I'd have had access to a book like this in early recovery. I'm still dealing with symptoms and this book is a Godsend. Not only does it provide great tools and reassurance, it also has a lot of information for carers, doctors and counsellors. If you have any experience with benzodiazepines then this book is an absolute must! Brilliant!"

~Peter A Davies, benzo survivor, Wales

BENZO-WISE

A Recovery Companion

*Everything you need to know to cope
successfully with benzodiazepine withdrawal*

REVISED EDITION

Bliss Johns

Campanile Publishing

Campanile Publishing LLC, Iowa, USA

ISBN 978-0-9823759-2-1

Author's Note

This book has been written expressly as my personal account of my experience with benzodiazepine dependency. Omissions, if any, are genuinely as a result of my residual cognitive impairment at the time of writing and for no other reason. Under no circumstances has anything been written with the intention to be malicious, slanderous or vindictive.

The contents are more factual and anecdotal than scientific. It is, however, a responsibly written comprehensive guide which will prove invaluable to anyone discontinuing a benzodiazepine, their relatives, doctors and other caregivers.

It is my sincere wish that this book will be a source of information and awareness, and that it will give courage and hope to many.

To my loving, indomitable mother,
Nell Johns-Frederick

Thank you for teaching me by example
how to harness my inner strength,
and for giving me my first mantra:
This too, shall pass.

Acknowledgements

I am grateful to so many people who were supportive of me during my withdrawal. Most were not physically present or even aware of my challenge, but their regular phone calls and loving conversations spurred me on. I was on my own and had to learn how to ask for and accept help. In doing so, I was able to experience the joy of gratitude.

For their kindness and unwavering support, I thank:

Iain Padwick and Zoe King, Mike and Jill, Marj and Abi Lasebikan, Colleen Newport, Jackie, Arlette, my nieces and nephews, Daddy, Irvine, Debbie Napier, Hart Edwards, Phyllis and Tony Gonzales, Aunt Yvonne, Michelle, Mark and the rest of the Frederick clan, Aunt Olive, Saran and the rest of the Johns/McLeish clan, Lesley and Al Spencer, Crimson and Leslie Ala, Derek Armstrong, Colin and Paula Tang Choon, Tony Sorhaindo, Marion Cooper, Madge Thomas, David Griffiths and Edna Pascaretta.

Thank you to Professor C Heather Ashton for kindly reviewing and approving the medical information included in this book.

I also thank Paula Kovaks, Peter Davies, Valerie Bell, Una Corbett, Anthea Young, Jenny Robinson, Geraldine Burns, Mick Behan, Ray Nimmo, Barry Haslam, Ross McConnell, Pam Armstrong, the late Dr Reg Peart and the late Colin Downes-Granger, and everyone else within the wider benzo community who support and encourage others by sharing their knowledge, experiences and expertise.

Thank you, too, to the circle of benzo friends in cyberland who teach us so much by sharing their experiences.

Finally, this book would not have been published without the loving attention and support of my dear friend, Renetta Burlage, who encouraged, advised and held my hand throughout. It is as much hers, as it is mine.

Contents

Preface

Withdrawing from a benzodiazepine can sometimes result in losses, isolation and feelings of being misunderstood and unsupported. The concept of a 'feel-good' book that would give an emotional boost during withdrawal came as a result of numerous requests from visitors to the *Benzo-Wise* benzodiazepine recovery website (now *Recovery Road*).

The site was started to log my progress from withdrawal through to recovery. As I shared more of my experience, I was asked to describe what the symptoms were like for me and how I coped. I soon started receiving emails from users who wanted permission to print the logs. Relatives and caregivers also began requesting written information to pass on to those too unwell and cognitively impaired to use a computer.

I have included practical information about benzodiazepines and withdrawal based on my experience, counselling training and chemical dependency research. The main focus, however, is on being emotionally safe and coping well.

Due to brain fog and other continued effects of the drug, cognition is often impaired and clarity, reading comprehension, concentration and memory can be affected. Asking the same question repeatedly and becoming confused by anything that is not straightforward is common in those going through withdrawal. With this in mind, I have assumed an informal tone throughout and have tried to devise a simple format. Any clichés and repetitions such as 'This too, shall pass' and 'Withdrawal is temporary' are intentional. I hope these modifications will have the desired effect of making this easy to read.

Introduction

I continue to receive emails daily thanking me for the information and reassurance this book is providing to users, relatives, doctors and counsellors. It was written with the primary intention of giving hope to anyone experiencing a troubling withdrawal, and so I am pleased and relieved that it is indeed fulfilling its purpose, and has even surpassed expectations.

What I am about to share next is extremely important and needs to be assimilated well, especially if you are reading in preparation for your taper. I had an intense withdrawal; you may not. There are people who have successfully quit benzos with very few problems; it is possible that you could too. These success stories are not found on the internet because those users had no reason to communicate online. You must always keep this in mind as you read my story or any other. If you don't, and you anticipate the worst, you will worry and become anxious about something that may never happen. It makes more sense to preserve this emotional energy instead.

On the other hand, if you have already tapered or are in the process and you are experiencing symptoms, you will agree that a problematic withdrawal can be, at the very least, upsetting. Discontinuance causes the nervous system to be in a temporary state of constant hyperexcitability. This often results in the most bizarre physical and psychological symptoms: from muscle pain, twitches, gastrointestinal problems to distorted perception, anxiety attacks and sleep difficulty. This can happen to someone with no history of psychological problems, as in my case where I was prescribed a benzodiazepine for a facial tic.

Finding as many positives as possible while the recovery process takes place can make a big difference to your withdrawal experience. Try to focus on accounts where people have success-fully tapered, rather than the more disturbing stories. If you have the support of family or friends, share information on benzodiaze-pines with them so they can have a better understanding of what withdrawal entails.

Using a technique that works well for you will be advanta-geous. It can be as simple as a breathing exercise or repeating a positive statement. Do it as often as you feel is necessary. Stock up on a few books that make you feel encouraged, movies that make you laugh and music that uplifts you. Try to use as many resources as possible to make your days lighter without becoming too preoccupied or obsessive; moderation is key. By the time this is over you will find that you have become an expert self-nurturer.

Although the word 'healing' is used frequently, benzo with-drawal is not an illness; it is a syndrome or cluster of symptoms that occur at the same time. The nervous system is in a temporary state of being excessively excitable and overly sensitive to stimuli. Unless there are pre-existing or concurrent medical conditions, this will be the only reason for your symptoms. When the recovery process is complete, the symptoms will subside.

Provided you are well-informed, when you experience a symp-tom, no matter how bizarre, you will know that it is withdrawal and not an isolated medical problem. If in any doubt, seeking medical advice to rule out other probable causes will provide peace of mind.

The most important thing to keep in mind is that as unpleasant and unsettling as it can be for many, withdrawal does not last indefinitely. Most people do fully recover and those who unfortu-nately experience a few enduring symptoms often consider them to be minor compared to the effects experienced while on the drug.

If you have discussed coming off a benzodiazepine with your doctor but feel daunted or overwhelmed by negative accounts of the withdrawal experience, please do not let this deter you. More than likely, the reason you want to quit is because the side effects are making you unwell and you feel worse than you were prior to taking it. It will be worth it. Remember, your experience could end up being less extreme and only mildly unpleasant. If you prepare yourself mentally and get your doctor to supervise your taper, your withdrawal should be manageable.

Never stop taking a benzodiazepine abruptly or what is referred to as 'cold turkey' as this can cause serious medical problems including seizures. Instead, taper slowly and stick to your schedule. Don't be tempted to skip a phase of reduction if the symptoms seem manageable. Be patient; it is better to have what may seem like a long taper than rush the process and end up in protracted withdrawal.

If symptoms appear while you are tapering off the drug, try not to resist them. Accept them for what they are: evidence that you are on the way to being benzo-free. This is the beginning of your recovery. When it is over, you will be able to celebrate having a clear, lucid mind and a quality of life that is much better than you could ever have imagined. The most satisfying feeling will be the sense of accomplishment, invincibility almost, and the relief you will experience when you begin to have periods of improved cognition and wellness. You will forget the negatives and savour being well. In the meantime, be as gentle with yourself as you possibly can.

❦1❧

A Faded Memory:
My Success Story

Life was good. Not only was my life good, it was charmed. I was introduced to the concept of our thoughts influencing what we attract into our lives in my early twenties, and had become an expert at manifesting unlikely opportunities and many pleasant experiences.

This was confirmed during the summer of 1997. After being commitment phobic for what friends and family felt was a ridiculously long time, I gave in to their subliminal pleas and the incessant ticking of my biological clock. At age thirty-four, I started affirming to meet my 'kind, loving, attractive husband'. I was finally ready. It was no surprise that a few weeks later I met Dylan. The following year, on Valentine's Day 1998, he asked me to marry him. I accepted.

There was just one problem. It seems insignificant now but was a source of bother at the time. For most of my life, from age four years, I had had a twitchy 'quirk' where my right eye would tic involuntarily. It was not always noticeable and despite the mild twitching I enjoyed a normal, active, happy childhood. As I grew older I became more distracted by the tics and explored every possible complementary treatment in an attempt to relieve them, but to no avail. By the time I'd met Dylan I had consulted chiropractors, physiotherapists, osteopaths, herbalists and different types of massage therapists. These approaches contributed to my wellness but did not have the desired effect.

As Dylan and I planned our wedding, I knew I had to find at least a temporary cure. The tics were mild and infrequent at the time but there was a ninety percent probability that my face would do its little dance in the middle of the exchange of vows. If that happened I knew I would become flustered and embarrassed. I was adamant about not letting the tics ruin the day and this is why I went to see my doctor early one wet morning in the spring of 1998.

He first prescribed an anti-epileptic drug which was much too potent for my mild condition. Within days I returned to let him know it was making me too drowsy to focus. He then prescribed clonazepam, a drug I had no clue was used as a tranquilliser or that there was a high risk of dependency associated with its use. It was a low dose and helped the tics initially, reducing them to a few daily. I was elated. I had found the miracle cure and our wedding day was going to be perfect.

My euphoria was short-lived however, as the tics soon returned, but this time more frequently and intensely. Once I realised the medication was no longer effective, I stopped taking it. A few days later, I had the most frightening involuntary movements. I quickly took a dose and the fitting stopped. I thought I had developed a form of epilepsy or other movement disorder when I had in fact quickly reached tolerance (when more of the drug is needed to be effective) and by quitting cold turkey instead had what was my first withdrawal reaction.

When the dosage was increased, I once again rapidly became tolerant and the tics returned with renewed intensity. For fear of having more seizure-type movements, I continued taking the drug. The wedding dilemma seemed imminent and one week prior to the big event, I shared my concerns with my new doctor. He prescribed a small amount of diazepam to be taken adjunctively with the clonazepam. By the time the nuptial day arrived, I was tic-free but also heavily sedated. Despite my being in a near-catatonic state, Dylan and I enjoyed a charming, country manor ceremony and an unforgettable reception with family and friends.

I did not take diazepam again until my taper. Sadly, my dependency on clonazepam had, within one year of my first prescription, become well-entrenched. I just did not know it at the time. I ended up taking the medication through repeat prescriptions for more than seven years. For most of that time I was in tolerance, gradually having more and more obscure complaints and minor ailments or, what I now appreciate, were withdrawal symptoms.

During the earlier years on the medication life was relatively normal. I worked diligently within the voluntary sector in the areas of domestic violence crisis support and counselling. I also completed two years of clinical psychotherapy training. But gradually everything became a blur: the fog descended on my brain, I became easily fatigued, emotionally anaesthetised, spaced out and absent-minded. Despite eating healthily and exercising, my weight gradually ballooned out of control. This baffled me but I still did not identify the drug as being contributory in any way.

I also had regular, dramatic visits to the local hospital emergency room. On one occasion, due to a lapse in concentration, I peered at a tube of super strong adhesive to see if it was empty and squirted it directly into my eye causing my eyelids to stick shut. My neighbour must have questioned my sanity when I banged on his door jumping up and down, shrieking like a psychotic cheerleader. "Rhys, Help! Are you there? Crazy glue's in my eye. I've glued my eye shut," I cried. He looked at me in horror as I tried to tug the lids apart. When we arrived at the hospital I was immediately seen in a special 'ocular super glue injury' cubicle. It was reassuring to discover that this was a common mistake. I had more accidents that led to emergency visits that year, all too embarrassing to share.

When my memory began to be affected and the brain fog became too severe, for ethical reasons and in the interest of my clients, I gave up counselling and went to do a less demanding but well-paying job. I made unsound judgements with dire consequences but still did not, at that time, make the link. Although I had a feeling of foreboding and was generally unwell, I had no idea that this was in any way related to the drug.

In an effort to regain control of my life, I started searching the internet for answers. I eventually stumbled upon my deliverance in the form of the *Ashton Manual*, also entitled *Benzodiazepines: How They Work and How To Withdraw*. This lifeline for benzo users is written by Professor C. Heather Ashton, Professor of Clinical Psycho-pharmacology at the University of Newcastle upon Tyne, England. It contains the most invaluable information on benzodiazepines. I recall the tears gently rolling down my cheeks as I finally identified the reason for my challenges. The following morning I took a printed copy to my doctor. He prescribed the diazepam required for my taper and I left feeling optimistic. I didn't know how long it was going to take but I knew I was going to be well again.

Not ever having had any type of psychological problem, I dismissed many of the symptoms listed as being only likely to occur in people who had anxiety or depression as pre-existing conditions. I had no preconceptions of what withdrawal would be like. I devised a quick recovery plan which included stocking up on B vitamins, magnesium, calcium, homeopathic tissue salts, melatonin, valerian and a few other supplements that I thought would help. I was going to accept the symptoms without resistance, give them no attention, say my affirmations as always, continue meditating twice daily and focus on wellness. I told myself that in a few months I would be fully recovered and will have forgotten about my benzo experience.

When the symptoms started to surface during my first taper attempt I was confident about my ability to cope, but when I started having involuntary seizure-type movements that made driving dangerous, I reinstated in order to be able to go to work. This also happened during my second taper attempt. I eventually gave up work and, as a result, lost my home. By this time I had already ended my marriage. The drug had impacted every area of my life.

As I weaned off the clonazepam during the summer of 2005, the withdrawal symptoms began to surface. I had already resolved to accept them without resisting and did my best to remain calm and assume the role of 'detached observer'. I felt that if I stayed focused on the fact that the symptoms were indicative of the healing that was taking place, anxiety levels would be kept to a minimum. I would have to cope only with the withdrawal-induced issues.

I continued meditating, used positive self-talk, affirmations, emotional freedom techniques (EFT), diaphragmatic breathing and every other coping strategy I was aware of while I witnessed what was happening to my mind and body. During the acute stage of withdrawal I could not sleep, eat, every part of my body hurt, tingled, twitched, and my perception was distorted. I was constantly dizzy, my senses were heightened, my eyes were glazed and glassy. I had abdominal pains with vomiting and diarrhoea and every other withdrawal symptom conceivable. If I had not had this experience, I would not have believed it possible for a prescribed drug to wreak such havoc. I recall looking in the mirror and thinking I looked like an illegal recreational drug user in detox. At times it was frightening, but I kept affirming: *I am recovering; I am grateful for my healing.*

By late February 2006, I had my first window of clarity - a brief period during which the brain fog lifted and many symptoms subsided. It was my first glimpse of the long forgotten lucidity that would return with recovery. I thought that withdrawal was over. I was thrilled and immediately started making plans to return to work. The timing was wrong however, and with my nervous system still in a fragile state, the symptoms returned within days.

A few months later, I had another period where the fog again lifted and many of the symptoms relented. It was soon followed by intense re-emergence of the symptoms. This pattern of intermittent 'waves' of symptoms and welcome 'windows' of clarity continued with the waves gradually becoming shorter and the windows lasting longer. My withdrawal period lasted from June 2005 to December 2007. For much of this time, apart from having to cope with the waves of dizziness, nausea and other symptoms, my memory was badly impaired. I kept a notebook with my address, national insurance (social security) number, the day the rubbish was collected and other important information. I felt like someone suffering from early onset dementia.

Having kept diaries and journals since my early teens, it was easy for me to write during withdrawal. At times it was all I could do. During one of those periods when the symptoms subsided, I started writing about my experience online. This has evolved into the *Recovery Road* website which now provides support and encouragement to thousands of people worldwide.

I have not had a resurgence of symptoms since December 2007 and now consider myself fully recovered despite having two residual issues. I consider them (hearing distortion and involuntary movements/dyskinesia) to be indicative of the final tweaking of my nervous system.

As my memory and other cognitive faculties improved and my clarity sharpened, I began to realise that I was much more unwell during the tolerance years than I had first thought. This is the reason I am extremely thankful that I am now benzo-free. To have my cognitive faculties back was worth every minute of withdrawal.

I recently enjoyed an extended period during which the involuntary movements ceased completely. This has been my first such experience since my taper almost four years ago, and although they have returned, I continue to feel a renewed calm in my nervous system. I am overjoyed at this new development. It confirms that, as I always thought, these involuntary movements are linked to withdrawal and will eventually go. I am still in awe of how resilient and self-healing our bodies are.

Enduring a challenging and protracted withdrawal can be empowering. I genuinely believe that having survived benzodiazepine withdrawal, I will undauntedly face future life obstacles and so I revel in this new sense of near-invincibility.

Now that I am feeling physically, psychologically and cognitively well and recovered, I am able to focus on promoting benzo awareness and giving responsible support to others in withdrawal. The bonus for me has been the *Recovery Road* website which is the most fulfilling and rewarding thing I have ever done. It has certainly been my affirmation come true: that *much good comes out of every situation*. Sometimes we are sent unexpected challenges; somehow we find the strength and courage required to cope. We can even learn a few life lessons along the way. I am grateful for my recovery and pleased that life is good again.

2

How Benzodiazepines Work

"**B**e careful, these pills will fry your brain." These were the words whispered by the wise, white-haired pharmacist as he handed me my final bottle of little beige pills. He did not know I was tapering after having taken them for more than seven years and that although my brain was not 'fried', my GABA receptors were badly in need of repair.

Some benzodiazepines are widely and successfully used in certain settings such as in hospitals as pre-medication before operations, as one-off treatment only for nervous patients before a dental procedure, and in the treatment of some forms of epilepsy and movement disorders. They are also used in the management of alcohol withdrawal as they work to alleviate delirium tremors. The *British National Formulary* (BNF), which is a joint publication of the British Medical Association and the Royal Pharmaceutical Society of Great Britain, recommends only short-term (two to four weeks) use of benzodiazepines in the treatment of anxiety disorders. It also states that the use of benzodiazepines for mild anxiety is inappropriate and unsuitable.

The following is a basic overview of how benzodiazepines work. In order to simplify the explanation, I have not mentioned the GABA-activated chloride channels or any details that some may find too cognitively challenging to assimilate at this time.

Benzodiazepines, including Ativan (lorazepam), Xanax (alprazolam), Valium (diazepam) and Klonopin or Rivotril (clonazepam), inhibit the activity of neurons in the brain. They work by enhancing the activity of a naturally occurring neurotransmitter or messenger, gamma-aminobutyric acid (GABA). GABA is the most important and widespread messenger in the brain. GABA receptors are large proteins. When we take a benzodiazepine, it binds to the benzodiazepine sites on the GABA receptors. This enhances the actions of GABA by making the cell even more resistant to excitation and causes a calming effect.

The pharmacological profile of benzodiazepines varies as there are different receptor subtypes and with selectivity they cause different effects: sedation/hypnotic (sleep-inducing), anxiolytic (anti-anxiety), muscle relaxant, anticonvulsant and amnesiac (memory disruption).

The brain also has excitatory neurotransmitters such as norepinephrine (noradrenaline), dopamine, serotonin and acetylcholine. While GABA's inhibitory activity is being enhanced, the activity of these neurotransmitters which are necessary for many essential functions including heart rate and blood pressure control, normal alertness, memory and emotional responses is reduced.

Long-term benzodiazepine use affects the GABA receptors and causes the benzodiazepine subunits to become down-regulated. This in turn results in a decrease in GABA function. When this drug which the brain has now become dependent on for enhancing GABA's calming activity is discontinued, because of the down-regulation of the receptors, the brain is left in a state of GABA-underactivity. These changes which result in the entire nervous system going into overdrive and becoming hyperexcitable, are reported to be the cause of the adverse withdrawal effects that many experience.

Half Life

When a benzodiazepine is taken on a regular basis, there is an ongoing process of drug absorption and elimination. The time it takes for half of the drug to be eliminated or for the blood concentration level to fall by half is known as the half-life. This may vary according to individual, particularly in the elderly.

A hypnotic or sleeping pill has a shorter half-life of less than twelve hours and it lessens or loses its effect during the day allowing the user to be alert and function normally. However, rebound anxiety may occur and this could cause day time anxiety. An anxiolytic or tranquilliser has a longer half-life and its effect will be more evenly spread throughout the dosage period.

When someone on a longer acting half-life drug misses several doses or abruptly discontinues the drug, it can take days before withdrawal symptoms surface. This is important to know as some people who stop taking the medication abruptly spend a brief period thinking that they will not have withdrawal symptoms only to be unpleasantly surprised days later.

For example, the half-life of clonazepam is 18-50 hours. This means that if the last dose was taken at 8:00 am on Monday, it could take up to 10:00 am on Wednesday (fifty hours) for half of the drug to be eliminated and possibly another two or more days before withdrawal symptoms are experienced. This is why when I first developed a tolerance to the clonazepam and stopped taking it, the withdrawal-related intense involuntary movements did not surface until three days later.

People who use benzodiazepines sporadically or users who take those with a short half-life can experience 'inter-dose withdrawal'. When this happens, they begin to feel withdrawal effects between doses.

Tolerance

When the receptors in the brain become habituated to the action of a benzodiazepine, more of the drug is needed in order for the desired therapeutic effect to be achieved. This often develops with regular use and is known as tolerance.

With addictive substances there is a need to keep increasing doses because of tolerance. This is why benzodiazepines are initially effective but successive increases in dosage are usually periodically needed in order for the required effect to be maintained. This, in turn, can lead to additional benzodiazepines being prescribed when a safe maximum dose of one drug is no longer effective. Another good example of drug tolerance is alcohol use where a new drinker is able to feel its effects after a glass or two but eventually, as tolerance sets in, will need increasing amounts.

Tolerance develops more rapidly with benzodiazepines with a short half-life such as a hypnotic or sleeping pill. When the drug loses its therapeutic effect, sleep patterns return to pre-treatment levels. Anxiolytics which have a longer half-life may retain their effectiveness for longer periods but tolerance is reported to develop within a few months of the initial dose.

With long-term use of benzodiazepines the body adapts physiologically to accommodate the drug. When tolerance develops or the drug is discontinued the body takes time to readjust. It is during this period that withdrawal symptoms are experienced.

Paradoxical Reaction

If a patient responds to medication in a contradictory or opposite way to what is expected, it is said to have had a paradoxical effect. An example of this is pain relief medication causing increased pain. Benzodiazepine treatment can sometimes result in paradoxical reactions in susceptible individuals causing an increase in anxiety, agitation, aggressiveness, hyperactivity, insomnia and exacerbation of seizures in epileptics.

Dependency or Addiction?

Many people who become dependent on benzodiazepines as a result of medical treatment (termed iatrogenic addiction) resent being labelled 'addict'. This is understandable as their drugs were prescribed for a medical or psychological condition, not purchased in a dark alley from a pusher. Most do not experience cravings, exceed their prescribed doses or steal to maintain their 'habit'. Furthermore, they are often the ones who broach the issue of discontinuance with their doctors.

Continued exposure to a benzodiazepine will inevitably result in physical dependence. Whatever the term used, the reality is that someone who is dependent on benzodiazepines feels compelled to continue taking them, often because of fear of the troubling withdrawal symptoms or a belief that the drug is helping in some way. Because of the connotations and stigmatisation associated with the word 'addict', the World Health Organisation (WHO) recommends 'dependency' as the expression of choice for people iatrogenically addicted to drugs.

3

The Basics

'Unbelievability Factor'

E ven people who were usually trusting of my judgement and cared deeply were sceptical about a prescribed drug having such adverse effects. Only after I recovered did they acquiesce with bewilderment and relief. This inability to grasp the complexity and possible duration of benzodiazepine withdrawal could be referred to as the 'unbelievability factor'.

If you are experiencing protracted withdrawal and your family, friends or carers insist it is not possible and that withdrawal does not last longer than a few months, please share relevant information from credible sources with them. Then consider your circumstances carefully before doubting yourself or coming to this conclusion. If you do, you could end up feeling that your symptoms are caused by some other medical condition. This could result in further heightened anxiety and your being misdiagnosed and treated for something that is merely a withdrawal symptom, one which will eventually disappear.

If you are experiencing physical discomfort and are concerned, it is advisable to see your doctor and even have diagnostic tests if necessary. As in most cases, they will be negative and you will be assured that your symptom is indeed due to withdrawal.

Another way of identifying withdrawal symptoms is that they would first have appeared either during tolerance when the drug stopped being effective, when you first started weaning off, or during or after your taper. Users of benzos with very short half-lives and those who take the drug erratically may also experience symptoms as part of interdose withdrawal. You may also find that they abate during your windows of clarity and resurface during the waves of withdrawal, often with other accompanying symptoms.

I was fortunate that when I observed my psychological symptoms I knew they were caused by nothing more than a nervous system that was temporarily in a state of chaos. I did not focus on the peculiar distortions and waited until after they subsided before mentioning them. I felt I would be at risk of being misdiagnosed with a mental health disorder.

If the floor or furniture appear to be moving or you experience any other bizarre form of distorted perception (which first surfaced during withdrawal), please wait until your recovery process is complete before considering psychiatric treatment. This is provided you feel emotionally safe. If you regard it as just another withdrawal symptom as you would the gastric disturbances, headaches and other physical symptoms, you will cope. Once you are able to remain in awareness while observing the symptom, knowing that it is impossible for your furniture to move unaided, you will manage well.

I certainly understand why anyone who has not experienced benzo withdrawal would have doubts. I recall my bewilderment when I first observed the acute symptoms, especially the distorted perception. I used to shake my head in disbelief and fascination thinking, *incredible, absolutely incredible.* Later, when I was becoming frustrated at the insistence of everyone including doctors that "It could not possibly be withdrawal," I reminded myself of how dubious I, too, had been. Another misconception was that I had quit cold turkey or had done a rapid taper as that is the only way adverse symptoms are experienced. This is not the case.

There is definitely an 'unbelievability factor' to the benzo withdrawal phenomenon. It is complex and can be a conundrum even to the person in the throes of the experience. If your symptoms are persistent, please keep reminding yourself that although withdrawal can last months or even years, it is temporary. While you wait for your nervous system to recover, try to find ways to nurture yourself and get the support you need. In this case, time really does heal, and you are going to be just fine.

Cold Turkey

Once the benzodiazepine's ill-effects are identified, the user's natural inclination is to stop taking the pills. This is referred to as quitting 'cold turkey'. One of the most frequently asked questions is whether or not taking this route is advisable. The answer is always an unhesitatingly gentle but firm, "No." Abrupt discontinuance of a benzo is dangerous and not worth the risk. Some people think that if they stop cold turkey they will avoid the long, unpleasant withdrawal associated with a slow taper. To the contrary, anecdotal evidence suggests that cold turkey withdrawal may result in protracted withdrawal. It can also cause seizures, withdrawal psychosis and other serious problems.

As mentioned earlier in my story, when I realised the medication was no longer effective I threw it away only to find myself convulsing quite intensely about three days later. This stopped once I reinstated. It is a classic example of what can happen if the drug is discontinued abruptly.

Many of our website users who have been subject to severe symptoms for long periods (in some cases more than two or three years) unfortunately were taken off their medication abruptly or weaned off of large doses over very short periods. The consensus is that it is advisable and much safer to do a slow taper. For anyone wanting to discontinue a benzodiazepine, please wean off gradually and have your doctor supervise your taper.

Tapering

There are different recommended methods of tapering. One of the most successful and widely used is the Ashton method, as outlined in the *Ashton Manual*. It recommends the use of diazepam (Valium) to taper off other benzodiazepines because it is more slowly eliminated from the body. Diazepam comes in liquid form and in doses of 10 mg, 5 mg and 2 mg which makes it easy to make very minute reductions in doses.

If you have decided to discontinue taking your medication, there are a few factors which will determine the duration and pace of your taper and how well you are likely to cope.

- If you are on a high dose, you will take longer to withdraw. The drug will be reduced in very small increments periodically in order to allow your body to readjust to the new doses at each stage of reduction.
- The tapering schedule should be used only as a guide. If you require a longer period to taper, you can discuss this with your doctor and adjust it accordingly.
- Many people use razor blades or the water titration method to make the smallest possible cuts. It is believed that the smaller the cut, the easier it will be for your system to adjust.
- Benzodiazepines differ in potency. If you are on a highly potent one you will need a longer time to reduce. If you are tapering using diazepam, your dose of diazepam will be higher. For example, I was on 1.5 mg clonazepam daily which is equivalent to approximately 30 mg diazepam;

someone on 20 mg oxazepam which is lower in potency, is on the equivalent of approximately 10 mg diazepam and would have a shorter tapering period.

- Your personal circumstances, overall general health, the stressors in your life, stamina and previous experience with drugs, if any, may also influence how you cope and determine the pace at which you can realistically taper.

Many people taking benzodiazepines are also on antidepressants. If so, withdrawing from the benzodiazepine first is recommended. It is important to note that antidepressants also have withdrawal reactions and need to be tapered slowly.

If you are faced with additional stress such as a bereavement, admission to hospital or other crisis while tapering, it is acceptable and in some cases necessary to remain on the same stage of the withdrawal for a longer period. It is also important to avoid increasing the dose at this time, if possible. Once your circumstances are more settled, a further reduction in dose can be made.

You will need the cooperation of your doctor. If using the substitution method, she or he will also be prescribing the diazepam required. Having a support system in place is advisable. It would be good if you had a reliable family member or friend who is willing to learn about benzodiazepines and withdrawal. The benzodiazepine forums online also offer guidance. It is extremely important that you set the pace for your taper and not feel rushed to complete it or have anyone pressure you into weaning off quicker than you're comfortable with. This time you are in charge.

Recovery Timeline

The average period of recovery for people who have been on the drug long-term is reported to be between six and eighteen months. Those with milder dependencies can take as little as one to six weeks. This is not always the case, however, because the withdrawal experience is unique and varies according to individual. No one knows or can accurately predict how long it will take.

Dosage or number of years on the drug are sometimes considered to be good indicators. Anecdotal evidence shows that there is a tendency for those who have been on high doses for many years to experience a longer withdrawal period than short-term users. Still, it is useful to note that a person on a low dose for months and one on a high dose for years can end up having quite similar experiences. All the doctors I consulted during withdrawal insisted that it does not last for more than a few weeks, six months at most. They were misinformed. Weeks, months or years, withdrawal takes as long as it takes.

If your symptoms are many and severe, it does not mean your withdrawal will last longer. Conversely, having fewer and less intense symptoms does not mean your withdrawal period will be shorter. There is just no proven pattern of healing. Also, if you are taking other medication, consuming alcohol, experimenting with supplements or over-stimulating and exerting yourself, this could affect the duration.

Windows of clarity appear early to some but this does not always mean that their withdrawal period will be shorter. I had my first window approximately eight weeks after completing my taper but symptoms persisted for two more years. Some people take a much longer time to have their first window but this does not mean their withdrawal period will be longer. Others have short, frequent windows which gradually increase in duration until full recovery. Some have little or no windows but may take the same or even less time to recover, with symptoms spontaneously and permanently disappearing.

Comparing your situation with that of a user who you know has been on a similar dose and tapering schedule will do more harm than good. Our bodies respond differently. Another important reason is that although you may have been on similar doses with the same tapering schedules and methods, you may not know the person's full circumstances. She or he may have less support, could have a pre-existing condition, be taking other medication, consuming alcohol, taking supplements or overstimulating in some other way that you are unaware of.

You may even encounter well-meaning ex-users who announce that certain supplements, forms of therapy, exercise programs, etc. miraculously accelerated their healing. Before you become excited at having the same results, remember how individual a process recovery is. For every 'remedy' that has supposedly helped a user, you will find others who have said it caused their symptoms to worsen. I still find this quite remarkable, but it is true.

There will always be this element of contradiction. To attribute one's healing, or symptoms for that matter, to anything specific will be debatable until formal research is done. How can we tell? Someone can start taking a supplement just at the time when full recovery was imminent anyway, or when a flare-up was poised to surface. Speculation makes no sense. There are too many varying conditions to come to conclusions. If you feel that whatever is recommended is worth trying, I genuinely hope it works for you. The best approach would be to expect any outcome when you do experiment, but remain optimistic.

Finally, no one can predict how long it will take to recover or how the process will unfold. What we do know is that managing withdrawal requires large doses of patience, non-resistance, and the wise application of coping techniques. These will certainly make the time seem shorter. If the process is taking longer than anticipated, it is because your resilient, self-healing nervous system needs more time to recover.

∽4∽

Symptoms

It may seem ironic that this chapter which is about symptoms, the very nucleus of the experience, gives only a brief overview. Because they can be baffling, complex, unpredictable and persistent, symptoms sometimes steal our focus away from recovery. It is easy to become fixated and spend many hours browsing for information, analyses and diagnoses. There were times when I had to drag myself away from my computer for fear of developing 'cyberchondria'. Too much information about symptoms can be overwhelming and may cause additional anxiety.

It is because of this tendency that I have limited the content of this chapter. The comprehensive A to Z list of reported symptoms which can be seen in the appendices at the back of the book, and the detailed journal entries throughout, provide adequate and more in-depth information.

We are already aware that the emergence of benzodiazepine withdrawal symptoms in a chronic user is a natural response to discontinuance, dosage reduction or tolerance. Yet, this does not prevent distress when the troubling symptoms surface, and even the strongest of characters may become apprehensive.

A pragmatic way of dealing with intermittent waves or flare-ups is to regard every single symptom as being present only because the nervous system is in temporary overdrive. It is the long-term use of the drug that has caused changes to the GABA receptors in the brain. Accepting that a myriad of symptoms may be present in varying degrees of intensity until these receptors are repaired will help significantly with coping.

For many users, one of the more challenging aspects of withdrawal is determining whether some of the bizarre things that happen to the mind and body are symptoms or dreaded diseases. Although I thought I was well informed about withdrawal symptoms, when I first had my perception distorted I was concerned. It was scary and I felt unprepared. Only after doing more research and finding further supporting evidence did I accept it. Receiving confirmation that the strange occurrences are indeed symptoms provides relief and reassurance. This is one of the reasons the websites and forums are so well utilised.

Please do not allow the following summary of my symptoms to deter you. They were experienced in clusters, and although at the time I felt as if my transition to the non-physical was imminent, I now think of them with pride that I coped so well. Since they are only symptoms and were all due to withdrawal, I have not analysed them or linked them to any diagnoses. Despite many also being symptoms of common illnesses and other conditions such as chronic fatigue syndrome, they are in this case, part of the withdrawal syndrome.

The most important thing while you read this is to keep reminding yourself that not everyone will experience all or many of them. For those who do, they may be less intense and last for a short period, usually during the acute phase.

Summary of symptoms I experienced:

Headaches, tight band around head, distorted visual, auditory and tactile perception, muscle pain, profuse sweating, intrusive thoughts, spasms and other involuntary muscle movements, gastrointestinal disturbances, sleep difficulty with nightmares, benzo belly, lethargy, skin rashes, heart irregularities, mouth and teeth pain, light and sound hypersensitivity, dizziness, tinnitus and various other anxiety-related problems.

Many of these were experienced during the acute withdrawal period and disappeared after four to six weeks. Withdrawal really does become a distant memory. If I had not journalised my symptoms, I would not be able to write about them now. I recall attributing *everything* that happened from the beginning of my taper to my recovery as being benzo-related. If I had lost an eyelash during that time I would have said, "Wow! Loss of eyelash is another symptom." No, please don't check your lashes; it is not!

If in any doubt about a symptom, please seek medical advice. When my left hand and fingers became numb, I had diagnostic tests to rule out other causes. They were all negative and confirmed that it was withdrawal. I was not surprised when the numbness eventually went away and my hand returned to normal. Consulting a doctor who is knowledgeable about benzodiazepines or is willing to read the *Ashton Manual* will reduce the probability of your being misdiagnosed.

Acceptance

Ample references regarding the importance of non-resistance have been made throughout this book. This is because acceptance is the most important requirement for efficiently managing withdrawal. To resolve to cope successfully without fully accepting the presence of the symptoms is unrealistic.

For some people, acceptance implies giving up, resignation or failure. In a benzo user's world, however, acceptance means less distress and minimal anxiety. It is the difference between barely surviving withdrawal and coping well. Imagine that you are on your way home. You know without doubt that you *will* arrive. You look ahead and notice there is a massive traffic jam. You are stuck. There is no way out but through. All you can do is resign yourself to waiting. This is benzo withdrawal.

If you can apply the same approach to your symptoms, you will fare much better than if you try to direct or control how your recovery process unfolds. As you become aware of your symptoms, try to go with the feelings without struggling or attempting to stop them. You may not be able to do this easily at first, but as you learn to observe your body's physiological reactions, you will find that you can make a mental note of what is happening without letting the fear overcome you. Even if your anxiety levels are extremely high, you can simply surrender; resolve to do nothing but be with the feeling of your hands shaking, heart beating fast, agitation or however it manifests.

Whenever I had an intense feeling of fear or impending doom, I would take deep breaths and talk myself through it without resisting: *"Okay, here we go again, it's back. Ah well, at least I know what it is. Hmm... Feels like I'm petrified but I'm not really. Wow, look how shaky I am. I don't need to do anything. I know what it is and it will soon pass."* It works; just don't fight it. You are not going to stop breathing, faint, fall or die.

It can take time and practice to become fully accepting. You may occasionally still resist the symptoms. This is normal as it is instinctive behaviour to struggle when a threat is perceived. The key is to not give up or become impatient with yourself when this happens.

Try to see your symptoms as little inconveniences – the cars ahead of you in the traffic. You will soon notice that with practice, even if at first you do give in and fight a particular symptom, you will eventually be able to choose how you respond. Yes, you are stuck with annoying and bothersome symptoms, but it is only a temporary set-back. You will make it home to recovery.

Withdrawal is literally healing in action. If you are able to acknowledge each symptom, no matter how disturbing, as necessary - evidence that your nervous system is recovering, you will be able to truly accept them. As some of our website users say when new symptoms appear or old ones resurface, "So, this is what it feels like to heal."

∽5∽

Managing
Psychological Symptoms

The physical symptoms, no matter how unbearable, are often less frightening than the psychological. If a person has a bloated, distended stomach which is sometimes painful (benzo belly) there are certain things that will be done intuitively to cope. Without giving it much thought, he or she may decide to wear loose or elasticated waists clothing and avoid wheat. Coping with the disconcerting psychological symptoms, however, is another matter.

Most of the website users have reported the psychological symptoms to be scarier. They find them distressing and regard them differently to the physical symptoms. Not resisting is understandably more challenging. If you are experiencing psychological symptoms, here is relevant information along with a few thoughts and suggestions which I hope will prove useful.

Brain Fog

Brain fog is the term used to describe cognitive dysfunction which causes feelings of mental confusion and lack of mental clarity. It is associated with difficulty concentrating or learning new things, problems with reading comprehension and memory impairment.

Phrases used to describe this symptom include:

~ *"Feeling like my head is enveloped in a thick cloud."*
~ *"I used to be good at getting my point across, now I can't complete my sentences."*
~ *"I can't figure out simple instructions."*
~ *"I think one word but say another."*
~ *"Feeling lost in a dense fog."*

Brain fog is one of the reasons many people in withdrawal are misdiagnosed. This could be due to the fact that it is also common in other conditions including chronic fatigue syndrome and fibromyalgia. It is also a symptom of heavy metal poisoning and one of the first things I did when I was feeling unwell but had not yet identified the benzo as the culprit, was to have my dentist remove all my amalgam (mercury-containing) fillings. They were replaced with composite ones but this did not make a difference. I don't regret having had the dental work done but to treat brain fog, the underlying medical condition has to be corrected. In our case it is benzo withdrawal syndrome and time is the only cure.

Attempting to accomplish simple tasks when coping with brain fog can be frustrating. As you wait for the recovery process to be completed, acknowledge that your limitations are temporary and try not to force yourself or struggle to do more than you are capable of. You will benefit though, from gently stimulating your brain by using word games, puzzles or reading a simple book. Keep a notebook to record relevant information, journalise your thoughts if you feel up to it, and find your best or peak time to do things that require concentration.

Brain fog was one of my most persistent symptoms. I remember in moments of doubt, wondering whether it would ever go. As I neared the end of withdrawal my clarity improved remarkably.

Had I not journalised my experience, I would now have very limited recollection of what life was like with a foggy brain.

Depersonalisation

With depersonalisation, there is a sense of detachment and disconnection, as if the person is an outside observer of his or her body or mental processes.

Phrases used to describe this symptom include:

~ *"Feeling like an alien in my own body."*
~ *"Feeling detached, in an unfamiliar space."*
~ *"Feeling lifeless, mechanical, foreign…"*
~ *"Observing myself acting a part in the movie of my surreal life."*

This depersonalisation experienced during withdrawal is not indicative of dissociative disorder or any other psychological illness. It is withdrawal-induced and, in that sense, is no different to muscle and joint pain, skin problems or any other physical symptom. As the nervous system begins to recover, the depersonalisation usually becomes less intense and eventually fades away completely.

One way of accepting this symptom can be to regard it as an important self-protecting tool. When you think about the stressors and psychological trauma that some are subject to during withdrawal, it would make sense that being detached and emotionless may, in the most unlikely way, lessen the impact. While the recovery process takes place, you may benefit from using positive self-talk and grounding exercises.

Depressive Thoughts or Low Moods

I hesitate to use the term depression to describe the feelings of helplessness, hopelessness, sadness, social withdrawal, lack of enjoyment in activities and other issues that present in some people who experience a difficult and protracted withdrawal. This is because these feelings are a combination of an organic reaction due to discontinuance of the drug and having to cope with the repercussions. Directly or indirectly, they are present as a result of withdrawal.

When these moods of hopelessness are overwhelming, there is an inability to conceive a positive thought, be motivated or proactive. This is when talking to someone about your feelings can help. A phone call to a helpline may assist in lightening your mood. You do not need to explain about withdrawal or justify why you feel the way you do; a good helpline worker will listen actively and without judgement. If you have the support of family or friends, you could share how you feel and ask that someone checks in with you regularly.

Interacting with nature can be uplifting too and you may find going for walks or a swim uplifting. External aids are valuable at this time and some people have found that while they cannot elicit a positive feeling, it can be triggered by a motivational or relaxation CD or book.

Derealisation

Derealisation causes one's perception to be altered resulting in a sense of being in a strange or unreal reality.

Phrases used to describe this symptom include:

~   *"Lack of emotional depth."*

~   *"Inability to be spontaneous."*
~   *"Feeling as if I am observing everyone and everything around me through a thick, hazy veil."*
~   *"Feeling distant, cut-off, spaced out and withdrawn from the world."*
~   *"Being in a dream, an almost trance-like state in an unfamiliar world."*

Like depersonalisation, this is a withdrawal symptom and nothing more. It does not need to be analysed or treated as one would in the case of a dissociative or other mental health disorder. Again, reminding yourself that it is a result of your discontinuing the benzodiazepine and that you should regard it in the same manner as you would one of your physical symptoms, will lessen any related anxiety.

Paranoid Ideation

Another bizarre symptom of withdrawal is a preoccupation with unfounded, suspicious thoughts. The person may read negative meanings into innocent remarks, perceive some form of threat or persecution, or have delusions that others are plotting against him or her. There is an expectation of being harmed or exploited and the person is hypersensitive to any form of criticism. Usually this symptom is not as intense in a benzo user as in someone who is schizophrenic, but it can still be a source of worry.

As is the case with the other psychological symptoms, these paranoid thoughts will disappear when the neurological balances are re-established. Accepting that the symptom is present and that it is a result of temporary changes in the brain, can help with coping. Also, being able to detach and observe any thoughts of perceived threats while acknowledging that they are irrational, should prevent inappropriate retaliatory behaviour.

Obsessive, Unwanted Thoughts

This can be the most distressing symptom for some, especially in cases where the thoughts are scary or repulsive. I am aware of individuals who were told they had obsessive compulsive disorder (OCD) only to later confirm that it was just a withdrawal symptom. The thoughts were withdrawal-induced, triggered by temporary neurological imbalances, and faded as recovery progressed. Despite knowing that an obsessive, unwanted thought has surfaced because of withdrawal, it can be difficult to accept it and not resist. Because it invades the mind and crowds out other thoughts, it can be an upsetting symptom.

Fighting the thoughts will not cause them to go away; attaching fear to the idea of having the thoughts or their content will intensify them. Accepting them as a symptom and acknowledging they are false is the first step. Then comes the mantra: *This is benzo withdrawal; this is not me.*

Some people use what is known as the 'thought stopping process' where they shout, "stop" in their heads and distract themselves with an activity such as a puzzle or word game. They do this to interrupt the obsessive process, not to stop thinking. Others simply refocus and, if the thoughts are out of character, switch to another thought: *I would never choose to have these thoughts; this is withdrawal, not me.* They then gently introduce an affirmation or self-talk such as: *My mind is sound and I am well.*

If you are having obsessive thoughts, try not to give them too much energy. Don't panic or even be surprised when they surface and don't dwell on the content or the fact that it is happening. See if you are able to place them into the same category as you would a skin rash or any of the other physical symptoms. These thoughts do not last indefinitely. We often hear from users who had this symptom and were surprised when it stopped. After, when they access it from memory, they are able to refer to it without having a negative reaction as they did when it was obsessive. They are pleased to discover that the fear is no longer attached to the thought.

'Rational Mind'

When these psychological symptoms persist, many end up with the most troubling thoughts and feelings. They fear that these bizarre symptoms may be permanent. I am always relieved when a website user refers to the 'rational mind'. Once I read the words, "But then my rational mind says it is the drug and not me," I know that that person will be able to cope more successfully than someone who is unable to make this distinction. Being aware that the thoughts and feelings are present because of withdrawal and are not solely emotional or psychological in origin makes a big difference.

When these thoughts overcrowd the mind, it can be challenging to access a train of rational thought. However, the rational mind is still there; it still exists. When, in the midst of all the fear thoughts, you happen to get an: *I wonder if this is because of my withdrawal?* or similar thought, it is from your rational mind. Here is where having a prepared monologue of positive self-talk or an affirmation can distract you and save you from immediately drifting back to the fear thoughts.

Imagine that you have been struggling with a stream of unwanted thoughts, for example, the dreaded: *What if my brain is permanently damaged and I never recover?* Then you notice that just one rational thought has eased its way in: *But this isn't me.* You immediately recognise that you have engaged your rational mind.

If you have your monologue ready you can use this gap to jump on the rational thought train: *Yes, these thoughts are not me. I did not have them before withdrawal. They emerged during my taper along with other symptoms. They will go along with all those other symptoms when withdrawal ends. This is definitely due to withdrawal and not me. My mind is sound.* This can be applied to general thoughts of concern about withdrawal or to the more intense obsessive, unwanted ones.

If you are having periods where your mind becomes over-crowded with paranoid or other unwanted thoughts or your perception is altered, I hope this will work for you. Your rational thought processes, remember, haven't abandoned you permanently. They will return either during the gaps, during your windows of clarity or when withdrawal is over.

The best way to cope with psychological symptoms which emerge at the time of tapering off the drug or during any stage of withdrawal is to quickly acknowledge that they are present only because of your temporary receptor damage. Although very distressing, they are common and should be regarded in the same way as the physical symptoms. In most cases, like the physical symptoms, they are likely to eventually go.

6

Acute Withdrawal

Acute withdrawal syndrome is reported to last from less than a week to one month with a peak at around the second week. It can be the most frightening period for anyone in withdrawal, even when warned of the possibility of the physical and psychological symptoms. It is almost as if the nervous system is mourning the loss of the drug and is in a state of shock. Actually, it is.

The first few months after my last dose of clonazepam were the scariest. It was my third attempt at weaning off and I thought I was prepared. As shared before, because I did not have pre-existing anxiety or depression I dismissed the likelihood of my having most of the symptoms mentioned. I was unpleasantly surprised.

I recall not sleeping for four consecutive nights when I neared the end of the clonazepam part of my taper. Apart from the insomnia, my other early symptom was a constant tight band around my head like it was being held in a vice grip, gradually being tightened. Then more symptoms including the intense involuntary movements surfaced.

During the first week I took magnesium, calcium, the vitamin Bs, valerian, melatonin and herbal teas at different times, but nothing worked. I even tried hypnosis and relaxation CDs for sleep. It didn't take long for me to accept that only time could heal the imbalances all those years of benzo use had caused. My nervous system was much too sensitive and in the end I just drank adequate amounts of water and waited it out. I used every coping technique I was aware of including positive self-talk, affirmations, emotional freedom techniques (EFT) and diaphragmatic breathing as often as I could and this distracted me and kept me grounded. I knew that what was happening to my body and mind was a result of my discontinuing the drug and considered it to be the beginning of my recovery. I did not allow it to overwhelm me and although I was scared, I somehow knew I would survive.

The following journal entries were written while I was in Houston, Texas. They give graphic descriptions of my experience around the time I completed the clonazepam part of my taper. As you read them, remember that I was in tolerance withdrawal for many of the almost eight years that I took the drug. This could explain why I had such an intense acute period. For some users this phase is only mildly problematic. They experience only a few symptoms and with much less intensity.

June 29, 2005

The Countdown

"My taper has been manageable so far. In another two and a half weeks I will be completely off the clonazepam. No matter what happens, there is no way I will be reinstating. If I do, I may as well give up on ever being well again. I want to get my cognitive faculties back. This is all that matters to me now. Just a few more months and I will be completely benzo-free.

I have not been feeling too well this week but I know I will cope. Whatever happens during withdrawal, I am going to be fine. I am not the first person to quit benzos. Those before me recovered. I will too. I can do this. I will do this. This is the beginning of my healing."

July 8, 2005

Weepiness

"For the first time in years, I am beginning to be able to feel again. To have this confirmation that the emotional bluntness is going is encouraging. I cried for most of this week. Luther Vandross died last Friday and Houston's *Sunny 99.1 FM* hosts have been playing his mellow ballads non-stop. I remember seeing him in concert in Maryland almost ten years ago. He was a legend. Every time I hear one of his songs, I burst into tears. It is so sad.

Then I just went online and read that Richard Whitely, the host of *Countdown*, one of my favourite quiz pro-grammes in the UK, recently made his transition. I will miss him too. I didn't personally know him though, so why have I been crying as if I have lost a family member? To make things worse, more than fifty innocent people have died in the UK train bombings. What an atrocity.

This is a breakthrough in my recovery. I noticed earlier, as the tears started flowing, that I could literally feel an un-familiar tug of my heart strings. After being on the drug for a few years, I forgot what it was like to feel this profoundly. I know I'm not only crying for Luther, Richard and the UK victims, I am crying for my mother and for every loss that occurred during my emotionally anaesthetised years. These flowing tears are like a rebirth. This is my release. I am okay. I will cry until there are no more tears."

July 17, 2005

Screaming Receptors

"The stomach cramps and loose stools have returned. The pain is excruciating. I feel as if I am going to pass out. I just drank peppermint tea and took two teaspoons of aloe vera gel. Placebo effect or not, it will go away.

I am soaking wet. I haven't stopped perspiring and despite the air conditioning, I look as if I recently showered and forgot to dry myself off. I am nauseous and have no appetite. My head is pounding and my eyes hurt. They look glassy, like a cocaine addict's. My joints hurt, my muscles ache and my legs feel like jelly; I can hardly stand. I have this crawling, stinging sensation on my skin. This is weird! All the teeth in my mouth hurt.

I have not slept for the last four nights. I can't tolerate light and sounds are exaggerated. My heart beats wildly echoing in my brain. I am jumpy and my head spins all the time, especially when I stand. Things seem to be moving all around me and my gait is unsteady.

This is scary. Well tough! I won't be taking any more poison. If I didn't understand what was happening to me I would have dialled 911 for an ambulance or checked myself into a hospital or mental health institution by now.

Despite everything, I am happy I know about withdrawal now. All these symptoms are normal according to the research I've done. Every time my stomach cramps or the pain becomes unbearable I affirm: I *am releasing, I am grateful for my healing.*"

July 25, 2005

A Little Less Intense

"I am lying down as I write this. Today is a little better. I slept for two hours last night and I've stopped throwing up. My stomach still gripes and my abdomen is swollen. The band around my head feels tighter and my eyes are glazed and shiny. They look as if they're popping out of my head.

This is scary because when I look in the mirror I'm seeing someone else. I am disconnected, as if this is not me. I feel as if I'm floating and I can only stand for a few minutes. When I do, I feel as if the floor is rising up to meet me.

My skin feels as if insects are crawling all over me, I'm still seeing flashing lights and I'm dripping wet almost all the time. Okay... calm down... breathe. You know what this is. Your brain is screaming for the benzo. That's all it is.

I feel like phoning 911 for an ambulance but dare not. They will definitely have me confined to a mental health institution. I will not panic. I will lie here and trust that these feelings will soon subside. In time my brain will readjust to this change. I will not give in. I will be brave. This is my healing. *I am safe. My mind is sound.* This is my chance to get my life back."

I endured these intense symptoms for at least another three weeks. I found strength, courage and determination that I never knew I had and managed to cope well. It was bewildering at times but I totally surrendered and accepted the symptoms. By this time, I had very little money left. I could not have afforded another month's rent and so decided to leave Houston.

August 27, 2005
At Six Weeks Off

"Tomorrow I will be leaving for the UK. The hurricane is heading for the Gulf. I hope everyone is safe and that there are no fatalities. Hope it doesn't affect the flights. Don't know how I will cope with the airport chaos but at least I am not vomiting any more.

I liked it here although I was isolated. I guess it was best for me to go through this part of withdrawal on my own. I cannot imagine any of my friends or family seeing me like this and not calling for an ambulance.

I feel totally disconnected and am still wobbly on my feet. I'm still fitting a lot but you know what? I'm going to make it safely home. I have always been divinely guided and protected and this is no exception.

I am grateful for the strength and will to be able to travel safely. Thank you for an incident free journey. *All is well. I am well.*"

When I wrote the following log, I was verging on wallowing in self-pity but was also determined to remain optimistic and not get into the victim mode. It sounds like a lecture but is a good example of positive self-talk.

October 8, 2005
Acute Withdrawal Is Over

"You have made it safely through acute withdrawal and that proves how strong you are physically and mentally. Remember to say "well done" and "thank you." This chapter is now closed.

Today I feel the need to remind you that this is a temporary situation. Do not let your current symptoms consume you and freak you out. Fear will weaken you and right now you need all your strength. I am not saying that you should pretend as if all is well. Actually yes, that is exactly what you need to do. Why? Because acting 'as if' will make you feel better, even if only emotionally. Do what is necessary on a practical level to be comfortable, then take yourself to a mental haven of vibrant health.

You are not a victim and benzo withdrawal is not a 'bad thing' that has happened to you. To the contrary, coming off the drug is the best thing that could have happened. This is what you need to celebrate. This is a blessing and many good experiences await you because of it. You are just unable to see the bigger picture at this time. You can visualise it though. It will keep you focused and this is what you need as your healing takes place, not fear and sadness.

When you write or speak about your symptoms frequently and for long periods you are expanding their influence. You are giving them more energy and power; no wonder you are becoming overwhelmed. You know better; focus on what you want, not what you don't want. View this experience as temporary, which it is, and give the negative aspects as little attention as possible. For every symptom you have, think of wellness. See yourself as you hope to be when you recover. Then you will be less anxious. Because you have changed your focus to all the good that you know awaits you, you become patient and non-resistant as your healing unfolds."

That was quite a severe rant but I felt I had to take drastic action to avoid depression. As intense as the acute phase sounds, it is manageable. Awareness and acceptance are useful coping tools and it allowed me to observe the symptoms while appreciating that it was the beginning of my recovery process. This was when I acknowledged the usefulness of being able to witness the symptoms as being part of the withdrawal syndrome and not individual medical or psychological disorders.

I admit that at times the symptoms were frightening. It was the first time I had experienced anxiety or distortion of my perception. More than anything, I was fascinated by the imbalances that resulted from my discontinuing the drug and the peculiar manifestations. Once the symptoms lessened in intensity, I exhaled. I did not collapse and die. I did not get up in the middle of the night, howling at the moon while running around Texas Medical Center, as I feared I would when I first experienced distortion of my perception. This was an organic reaction and nothing more; my mind was sound and my recovery process was on schedule.

∽ 7 ∽

Post-Acute and
Protracted Withdrawal

Protracted withdrawal syndrome is much more common than currently acknowledged. It involves the most complex symptoms which, as we are aware, are the direct result of drug-induced changes to the brain's receptors, as well as the manifestation of indirect effects of long-term use of the drug.

This syndrome can linger for months or even years. When symptoms persist longer than eighteen months it is considered to be protracted. Complaints can be as vague as flu-like symptoms or a combination of pathologies mimicking chronic fatigue syndrome, lupus, multiple sclerosis, anxiety disorders, irritable bowel syndrome and other chronic conditions.

Common to this phase of withdrawal are periods where the symptoms gradually lessen in intensity or abate totally only to resurface intermittently. As you already know, these recurrences are often referred to as 'waves' and the periods of reprieve, as 'windows'.

The following logs were written during my post-acute and protracted periods. At the time of writing the first entry, I did not understand the concept of waves and windows. I thought that withdrawal was finally over. This was a very brief window and the symptoms soon returned.

The early part of the post-acute period was profoundly challenging. When I reviewed the journal entries, I could see how much they reflect the thick brain fog and incoherence I was experiencing at that time. Although most are disjointed and uninspiring, I hope they will give further insight into the dynamics of this complex recovery process.

February 26, 2006
My First Window

"Today the veil has been gently lifted and everything is bright and glowing. The sun is emerging after what seems like years in another universe. I am filled with hope and a knowing that withdrawal has at last ended. I feel like a new person.

This is overwhelming. I cannot recall being this lucid since the late 1990s. It feels great to be able to feel again, to connect with myself and others, and to have energy to do the little things that were impossible to do just a few days ago.

I am so grateful for my healing. It has been a long time but my precious brain has finally readjusted to being without the dreaded pill. Thank you. Thank you. Thank you."

July 8, 2006
Patiently Waiting

"It was bad timing. I had my follow up consultation with the neurologist earlier this week and was in the throes of withdrawal. When I saw him at the end of February, the symptoms were less intense. I mentioned withdrawal and he said it does not last this long. This time I didn't say anything. I was perspiring profusely, my hands were visibly shaking, and I know I looked like I should have been immediately admitted to their psychiatric wing. I could sense his concern as he observed the symptoms. When he asked if I would be willing to see a neuropsychiatrist, I knew there was no way I could justify declining.

What is going to happen to me if no one believes that this is benzo withdrawal? I don't know how much longer the symptoms will persist. It has been eleven months since my last dose of clonazepam, and almost six since my last diazepam. Apart from the usual symptoms, the light and hearing sensitivity is intense. Barely managed to watch *Wimbledon* and every sound freaks me out. I thought I would have been back at work by now but there is no way I could cope with even a part-time job. I can't believe how persistent these symptoms are. This is unfathomable. All I can do is wait."

August 29, 2006

Recovery on Schedule

"I still cannot tolerate the computer screen for long; I can't focus to read either. It doesn't matter anyway, because with this impaired cognition nothing makes sense. Somehow I can cope with staring mindlessly at the television screen and it is now my new companion. I watch everything and cannot miss the *Friends, Frasier, Keeping Up Appearances* and *Seinfeld* reruns. They make me laugh.

There is nothing I can do but accept that I need to allow whatever my nervous system deems necessary to unfold. This is a great lesson in patience for me. Fighting what is happening won't make it go away. I will keep reminding myself that I am getting better, even if at times it doesn't seem apparent. My recovery is right on schedule."

September 9, 2006
Happy Birthday Mum

"The path of least resistance is ahead of me. It is the only one I can take while I observe my nervous system in overdrive and shake my head in disbelief. Today would have been Mummy's birthday. I miss her. If she were here she would have put her arms around me and said, "Darling, this too, shall pass." Yes Mum, I know my healing is taking place. This is why the symptoms are present. *I relax, I release and I let go.* You are right, this *will* pass."

December 20, 2006
Quiet Christmas

"It's been a long year. I am starting to have a few more windows and have accepted that my recovery is on schedule. I have been benzo-free for a year and although it has been a challenging one, I have no regrets. I know I'm going to be okay. This will be a quiet Christmas. I'm going to be alone but of my own volition. Coping with gatherings and other festive events is too much for me at this time. My friends and family understand my need to be on my own. I have been fortunate in this regard. A few days ago I had a little window but another wave is here. The fog is too thick for me to write more."

March 29, 2007
A Spring Window

"The long wave has ended and I am enjoying another window. I love these windows because they give reassuring glimpses of recovery. I have stopped anticipating waves or windows. It has taken me this long to learn about relinquishing control. True power lies in totally surrendering.

Now I tell myself that if another wave comes it is because it is meant to, and if this window lasts indefinitely it is also because it is meant to. I can't control the recovery process. I can only accept that whatever emerges is a necessary part of my healing.

Today, I shall enjoy this window. I won't worry about resurgence of symptoms or anything else. Spring is here. I will sit in the garden and watch the swans and ducks glide by. This is a good day. *I am grateful for my healing.*"

June 1, 2007

Another Wave

"The past few nights have been weird. I guess I'm having another wave of residual symptoms as I'm unable to sleep for more than twenty minutes at a time because the involuntary muscle movements keep waking me up. I've tried chamomile tea and drops of lavender on my pillow. They don't seem to be helping. I'm doing all the right things I think - comfortable temperature, dark room, no television or other stimulation, but to no avail.

I am tired. I know this will pass so I won't get too stressed. When I can't sleep I do my diaphragmatic breathing and repeat a few affirmations. Then I doze off again until another spasm wakes me up.

Despite everything, I am still grateful that I don't have the numerous symptoms that I had a year ago. *I am grateful for my healing. All is well. I am well.*"

June 5, 2007

Walking the Talk

"This recent wave of withdrawal has certainly been a test for me. It has been a challenge for me to follow my own advice. So often I've written about being patient and gentle with oneself yet I've spent the last few hours disturbed by the resurfacing of the distended abdomen, dizziness and other symptoms. It has been the most intense wave within the past six months.

I was looking forward to resuming my normal activities. The resurgence of these symptoms means I have had to cut down on the exercise routines I started when the last period of clarity began. I've also had to make other lifestyle adjustments such as eliminating wheat from my diet because of the benzo belly.

What can I say? I have a choice. I can remind myself that this angst will only contribute to my discomfort and refocus. I will think of how much better I am than a few months ago, of how fortunate I am to be over the worst. I will affirm my wellness with the knowing that I have already received my healing. I will see all the good in my life now and that good will expand. *I am grateful for my healing. I am well. All is well."*

June 26, 2007
Challenging Wave

"The current wave of withdrawal is finally receding. It started with the distended abdomen, progressed to severe dizziness, and profuse sweating and ended up with me spending the last ten days under my duvet with chills, sweats, tooth and gum pain, brain fog, joint/muscle pain, and almost constant spasming.

This wave lasted a full month. It was the longest since December's. I am shocked that the symptoms could be so intense this long after discontinuing the drug. Such is the nature of benzo withdrawal. This is a true example of the uniqueness of each person's experience.

It gets better though and eventually the waves will decrease in frequency until they stop recurring. For now, I am looking forward to enjoying this window of clarity with the hope that it will remain open indefinitely. Who knows? I am patient with myself and all is well. *This too, shall pass.*"

July 19, 2007
The Long Road Turns

"Today has been another good day. One of the good things about this experience is my new ability to take each day as it comes, to be patient and to go with the flow. I used to be a go-getter, 'monitor the process and ensure the result' kind of person. Now I can let go and trust that the outcome will be for my highest good without knowing how or when.

When I had my last wave of withdrawal, I reminded myself of the fact that when we set out on a long journey by car along an unfamiliar winding road, we can only see a few hundred yards ahead at a time. Yet we trust that we will get to our destination and more often than not, we do.

Sometimes, when it seems that this benzo journey will never end and frustration, desolation and anxiety threaten to take over, trust that you are on the right track. You will reach your 'fully recovered benzo-free' destination when the timing is right. Even the longest road has a turning."

This window lasted a week and was followed by another long period of more unrelenting symptoms which abated briefly in late August.

September 2, 2007

I Am Well

"Today has been one of those days. I've been having a few withdrawal reminders but nothing to make me think another wave is approaching. I haven't had the classic profuse sweating or mouth/teeth pain so I'd be surprised if what I'm experiencing lasts longer than a few days.

My current symptoms include joint stiffness and muscle pain, especially those in my back. So I'm taking my own advice and having some 'self-nurturing bordering on totally indulgent' time-out.

I know I will be fine soon. As I always remind myself, this is nothing compared to even six months ago. I will continue to give thanks for my healing. *I am well. All is well.*"

September 5, 2007

Benzo Belly and More

"More withdrawal symptoms have surfaced over the past few days. The benzo belly is back and I look as if I'm about to give birth. My body feels very, very heavy. A slow walk up the stairs is leaving me breathless and tired. I literally flop on the bed where I have to rest for a while before attempting to move again. I've also been having chills, sweats, dizziness and the nausea is back. The spaciness, brain fog and other head stuff have also resurfaced.

What can I do? Often, when a wave of withdrawal returns, I am tempted to question whether or not something else is wrong. If I did not have my windows, I know I would be even more doubtful. But I am glad I have not had the dreaded mouth and teeth pain. I am dealing with the other symptoms by resting, eating sensibly, listening to soothing music and being patient.

This morning I reminded myself that this is just another wave which will soon pass. Nothing I say or do will accelerate my recovery and the more agitated and impatient I become, the less likely it is that I will feel well, even if only emotionally. *This too, shall pass. I am grateful for my healing and all is well.*"

September 22, 2007
Our Essence

"We are never given more than we can handle." This cliché came to mind today and although it is often overused, it is true. The mere fact that we are still here, still hopeful and healing (which we are even if it seems like it is taking forever) is confirmation of this. Then I thought, to be 'given' benzo dependency and withdrawal must mean that we are inherently strong enough both emotionally and physically, and courageous beyond measure. No matter how shaky, fragile and traumatised we may be feeling as we go through withdrawal or its aftermath, we must remember this and acknowledge this part of ourselves that we can never lose.

At the core of our being is our essence. This has remained unchanged and unharmed from the benzo and will once again become apparent. It is who we really are and to over-identify with our symptoms means we could end up forgetting our true selves. It is good for those of us going through withdrawal to spend time reminding ourselves of our core qualities, the ones that may not always be evident during withdrawal but we know are still there and always will be."

September 26, 2007

Hope

"Hope is a good thing, maybe the best of things, and no good thing ever dies" is a quote from one of my all-time favourite movies, Stephen King's *Shawshank Redemption* (1994). It is so easy to lose hope when a situation takes longer than anticipated to be resolved, or when our egos interfere in our healing by trying to control the process, as in how and when. The key then, I tell myself, is to let go and not have a timeline or other expectation. I can use what I have now, today, to be comfortable and make my life as pleasant as possible.

This was my gentle reminder this morning after waking up feeling spaced out with a few other benzo reminders which I am choosing to ignore. Instead, I am about to curl up on my sofa and watch *Shawshank Redemption* for the umpteenth time. *Today is a good day.*"

October 4, 2007

Non-Resistance

"I am now being reminded of how remarkable our bodies are as I can literally feel the recovery process taking place. It seems as if the tooth and mouth pain is gone for good. It did not resurface during the last two withdrawal waves and has been replaced with a constant tinnitus and intensified dizziness. I am beginning to get that sense of my entire central nervous system being readjusted and re-tuned.

Along with the tinnitus and dizziness I am having other symptoms but I won't give them much energy. Instead I am honouring my loyal body for coping with these new 'surprises' as well as the unrelenting ones.

For those of us in protracted withdrawal, making a conscious choice to not resist the symptoms and to accept them as being a part of the healing process really helps. At least it does for me and I hope it will for you too. As I write this my head is spinning but there is this voice inside saying, "It's okay, just be grateful for your healing."

October 8, 2007
Healing Reflection

"Always know that no matter what you are going through, at your deepest level the essence of who you are still exists. Irrespective of the drug's effects that have resulted in temporary challenges, you remain that special person who entered this world as a beautiful, healthy baby. Even if recovery is seeming to take a long time, always remember that your situation is temporary.

Know that despite your symptoms, your body is restoring itself to its natural state of good health and wellness, even while you are reading now. These recent experiences will only strengthen you and teach you valuable life lessons.

No matter what your symptoms are or what your life is like at present, when you are healed you will resume a fully functional role as parent, spouse, friend and most of all, a strong, resilient you. No one can take your place, that assigned space that only you in your own special way with your unique experiences can fill. Although you are currently facing these challenges, the special purpose that you came here to fulfill is unfolding.

Remember this during any times of doubt - how good it is to still be here and what a precious gift you are. Take time to see that every day, in many ways, you are fortunate. Gently let go of any concerns about whether or not you will heal and choose to find peace in your situation as it is now, today.

Take a deep breath, exhale, and relax into that warm, tender feeling of knowing that all is well and that your recovery is taking place. *This too, shall pass."*

October 23, 2007
Shell-shocked

"Today has been a funny one. I don't know why, but I feel shell-shocked. Occasionally I become overwhelmed with this whole benzo issue. I think because I have not had a good window of clarity recently to replenish my emotional reserves, I feel a bit numb.

I know this hiatus won't last long. I now understand the concerns of some of my friends here who have not yet had any windows. To go for such a long period with depersonalisation, derealisation and other psychological and physical symptoms must be daunting. If I, who have had quite a few windows, am finding this prolonged wave to be so challenging, I can't begin to imagine how they must feel.

Anyway, this is when we have to remain hopeful and also make the best of now. I keep reminding myself of all the encouraging stories I have heard of people who resumed normality post-recovery. The darkest hour is just before dawn. December 17 will be two years since I completed my full taper. Many people find that during the third year the nervous system begins to settle down and the receptors regain their affinity for attracting GABA; others have to wait a bit longer. In the meantime, I will make the best of today knowing that every symptom I experience is indicative of the healing that is taking place. *I am grateful for my healing."*

November 12, 2007

Feeling Better

"Soon I will be two years completely benzo free and, oh, how much better I feel compared to this time last year. I can only encourage anyone who is still experiencing withdrawal to try to let go of anxieties about your recovery. It is taking place now, even while you are reading this. At this very moment, bad symptoms or not, windows or not, you are getting better. Your nervous system is recovering and you are healing. The windows will begin to appear, then they will keep getting bigger, brighter and clearer until one day they become an open door ushering you into a world of mental, emotional and physical good health and wellness."

November 16, 2007

Yet Another Wave

"Today is an 'under the duvet' day. Somehow, the symptoms are back, especially the spaced out feeling and dizziness. I feel so strange. Everything seems dull and dark. I feel heavy, exhausted and lethargic, although I've done nothing. Really, how much longer can this go on?

I'm not feeling sorry for myself, just petulant. This is when I have to remind myself to be patient and trust that the healing is taking place, even though it may not feel that way. Ah well, such is the nature of withdrawal. All I can do is say more affirmations, nurture myself and wait. *This too, shall pass.*"

November 30, 2007

Another Window

"I am experiencing another beautiful window and it is reassuring. Am beginning to get a clearer picture of what benzo recovery will be like. To elaborate, for those who have not yet tapered or experienced windows of clarity: It is like getting lost in a fog for a long, long period, then going through a tunnel and emerging to find yourself in a beautiful garden. The flowers are bright, the sun is shining, skies are clear blue, and birds are singing; emotions you had forgotten existed are threatening to overwhelm.

I had a meeting midweek and was pleased that I was coherent and lucid enough to concentrate. Now, with the abating of many of the symptoms, I am better able to assess what life post-benzos may bring. I know I am not totally symptom-free as the distorted hearing, muscle spasms and a few others are still present. However, compared to how I felt during the recent unpleasant wave of symptoms, this is pure bliss.

The best thing about having a window, apart from feeling much improved, is that it contradicts what the well-meaning doctors and other doubters have said. If what we are experiencing is not benzo-related, why is there a pattern? Why do most of the symptoms surface in clusters and why do they re-emerge, intensify, abate or completely disappear at the same time? And why did they appear at the time of tapering off the benzo? I am grateful for these windows; they keep me hopeful."

Progress Reports

If you are frustrated because you anticipated a much quicker recovery, you could benefit from doing a 'progress report' or what could be referred to as a little comparison exercise.

Whenever I felt discouraged or concerned about the symptoms persisting for too long, or subsiding only to return in waves, I would remind myself of my pre-taper and acute withdrawal days.

Then I would think of my progress during the post-acute withdrawal months. It never failed to put my recovery into perspective.

I would think of how spaced out, how lethargic, zombie-like and unfocused I was, along with the host of other issues that made me go online to find out what was wrong with me in the first place. This would make me appreciate my decision to discontinue the drug, with absolutely no regrets.

I would then think about the unpleasant acute withdrawal months and that was enough to lift my energy. Acknowledging that the vomiting, weird perception distortion and other psychological symptoms were gone was all I needed to do to appreciate the progress I had made.

Then I would think back to the previous three or six months. I would be pleasantly surprised that many of the symptoms were no longer present. I remember feeling thankful that I was so much better. I would congratulate myself for coping and for making it through the worst part of withdrawal.

Finally, I would reassure myself that if I survived those months and had made such significant progress, then I could only imagine how well I would feel in another six months.

Sometimes there is an inclination to get immersed in thoughts of doubt which causes us to forget the progress we have made. This preoccupation makes us focus intensely on the remaining symptoms and it can test our patience and fortitude, making us scared and desperate.

These thoughts are fuelled by fear and this is when it is necessary to remind yourself that benzo withdrawal is temporary, that every symptom you experience is present because you have discontinued the drug. There is not enough binding of GABA to your receptors to calm your nervous system so it is temporarily hyperexcitable. Your GABA receptors must be repaired in order for you to recover.

If you acknowledge a symptom as a necessary part of your re-covery - evidence that it is taking place - you may end up feeling less resistant. You will then be able to accept that you are weeks or maybe a few months away from full recovery. You will know that you are in the process of regaining control of your life. This was the reason you decided to discontinue the drug in the first place.

I recall wondering if my protracted withdrawal would ever end. Today, I can hardly remember what it was like. It will be the same for you.

❦8❧

Coping Tools

One of the most successful strategies for coping with benzo withdrawal is to make the decision prior to or early on in the tapering process to accept the symptoms without resisting and to use techniques found to be most effective for self-management. Attitude can make a significant positive difference during withdrawal. I have seen people with very high anxiety and numerous physical and psychological symptoms cope better than others with very few symptoms and reportedly lower anxiety levels. This is because they are non-resistant and use as many tools as possible to manage their symptoms.

Quite often, the withdrawal-induced combination of low, depressive moods and anxiety results in an inability to feel motivated. The user is void of energy and unable to initiate positive self-talk or any other anxiety-reducing approach. When this is the case, the use of external aids such as relaxation CDs, regular grounding and breathing exercises can elicit favourable results.

There are, however, a few important factors to be considered. Depending on how severe withdrawal is, it can be challenging to focus long enough to learn something new, especially if cognition is affected. Also, some people are emotionally and mentally fragile and report feeling raw, exposed and vulnerable; they may find some techniques to be too emotive. In such cases, caution should be exercised and only the simplest and most appropriate ones should be attempted.

Emotional safety is key at this time. If you live alone and are unsupported, or if you are experiencing intense depersonalisation, derealisation, adrenaline surges, feelings of impending doom, distorted auditory, visual or tactile perception, organic fear or other psychological withdrawal symptoms, you may want to try a simple practice instead. You could try focusing on your breath or talking yourself through the symptoms. If you plan on attempting a new technique which requires a consultation, please ensure that it is with a qualified, licensed practitioner and that you have safe and adequate support.

The following are reported to be of use during withdrawal. They help with anxiety and stress-related issues. Some are also good techniques that can be used post-recovery especially in cases where anxiety was a pre-existing condition. Not all of these will resonate or be suited to you but through trial and error you could end up finding a few safe, reliable methods which will help you to manage your symptoms.

Affirmations or Positive Self-Talk

A most powerful coping tool which can be used during withdrawal is the use of affirmations or positive self-talk. How you speak to yourself during withdrawal can strongly influence how well you will cope. Being aware of your inner dialogue and gently changing a negative thought to a constructive and positive counter-thought is a good way of remaining optimistic.

I started consciously using affirmations in the mid 1980s after reading *You Can Heal Your Life* by one of the founding mothers of the self-help movement, Louise Hay. I soon found that it was the most simple and enjoyable way of changing what I attracted into my life. I later did a course to be certified to teach how to use them.

Contrary to what some believe, there is nothing 'new-agey' or mysterious about affirmations. Everybody uses affirmations every day, whether we acknowledge that we do or not. A thought of concern is as much an affirmation as any of the positive statements. Repeatedly saying or thinking: *This symptom just won't go away,* or *My withdrawal is not ending,* are classic examples.

If nothing else, on a cognitive level, affirmations drown the worry thoughts and make room for more positive ones that fuel health and well-being. Even if you are unable to connect with your feelings because of emotional bluntness, instead of the energy going to thoughts of fear and dread, the focus will be on your healing and you will benefit.

By the time you've repeated a few affirmations, you will notice an energy shift and the fear will be replaced by a knowing that you are going to be well again. Despite the symptoms being present you will be responding differently. This is because you are now in alignment with how you want to feel rather than being overwhelmed by how you do not want to feel. It is powerful.

It is okay if a positive affirmation sounds feeble and unconvincing in the beginning. If you are having unrelenting physical or psychological withdrawal symptoms you may think it is not realistic for you to proclaim yourself 'vibrant, healthy and whole'. Coming to this conclusion and dismissing the idea of affirming is normal. It is still worth exploring, however. You may be pleasantly surprised, and not with negative side-effects. You will find that in spite of how you may be feeling, if you continue saying a positive statement, you will eventually sense a shift in energy and gradually get to the point where you begin to believe that it is possible for you to at the very least be on your way to becoming 'vibrant, healthy and whole'. This is how affirmations work.

Try to get into the habit of noticing your thought patterns - not obsessively - just gently being aware of the worrying, anxious ones. (This works for withdrawal-induced thoughts as well.) Once you identify thoughts straying towards the symptoms, concerns or other fears, you can gently acknowledge them and, without judgement, say something such as: *"It's okay that I'm having these thoughts. I also know that every day, in every way, I am getting better and better."* Then you continue with: *"Every day, in every way, I am getting better and better"* or *"I am vibrant, healthy and whole."*

Everyone can enjoy affirming good. You can say affirmations periodically throughout the day - whatever feels right for you and as often as you like - the more frequently, the better. You can say them in front of the mirror or write them down; if you have a journal or notebook and feel up to writing, you can allow yourself to get carried away. The key to getting the best effect is saying them with emotion, conviction and resolve. In addition, visualising yourself fully recovered and imagining what it will feel like will create a more powerful shift in energy.

It is best to stick to one or two affirmations and not do too many at once; keep it simple. Less will produce more focus and the more often you repeat one statement, the easier it will be for the affirmation to begin to ring true.

Affirmations work; you do not need anyone's approval or to justify or scientifically prove this. All you need to do is use them to create good in your life. Keep your affirmations private or say as little as possible. This can be your secret project. When others notice the positive changes, they will ask, "What have you been doing?" It is inevitable.

Here are a few affirmations. You can also make up your own. Affirm only what you want and don't mention the symptoms; the focus is on wellness.

- ~ *'My body is self-healing and restores itself to perfect health.'*
- ~ *'Every day, in every way, I am getting better and better.'*
- ~ *'I am vibrant, healthy and whole.'*
- ~ *'I love and approve of myself exactly as I am.'*
- ~ *'My mind is sound and my body is healthy.'*
- ~ *'I am grateful for my wellness.'*
- ~ *'Every cell in my body is renewed; I am perfectly healthy.'*
- ~ *'Wellness is my natural state of being.'*

Sometimes it can be challenging to believe that such a simple technique can be so powerful. The mind is indeed powerful and it is good that we can choose our thoughts. As you begin to explore the use of affirmations and they start to feel 'right', you will feel lighter. A fun element will creep in where you end up enjoying using them in every area of your life.

Breathing

Even if nothing else works for you, finding a good breathing technique will have a positive influence and help to calm your nervous system. You will be equipped with one of the most natural tranquillisers for the nervous system.

Overbreathing during withdrawal

Overbreathing or hyperventilation occurs when one breathes deeper or faster than is necessary, often as a result of stress or anxiety. It is also a classic occurrence for many in withdrawal. Breathing is natural and many people are unaware of their patterns. When a person overbreathes the body does not have enough time to retain the carbon dioxide; he or she ends up having too much oxygen but is unable to utilise it due to this lack of carbon dioxide.

This can cause many problems including light-headedness, palpitations, shortness of breath, dizziness, headaches, numbness and tingling in extremities, chest pain, sweating and even fainting. If you become aware that you are overbreathing there are several things you can do:

Use a paper bag or a similarly expansible container and breathe in and out of it. This will force you to regulate your breathing and re-inhale the carbon dioxide which you need.

Do some form of exercise like walking on the spot or going up and down the stairs – whatever is comfortable for you. If your withdrawal permits, try exercising regularly (even short walks outdoors) as this is good and can help to reduce the likelihood of recurrence.

Practise any of the following breathing techniques:

The simplest way to start is by letting your mind gently focus on your breath as you take air in and out slowly. You will begin to create a rhythm as you become more aware of your breathing pattern and it becomes steadier.

3-3-6 Breathing

An uncomplicated exercise which can be used to create a rhythm is to breathe in to the count of 1-2-3, pause 1-2-3, and slowly exhale through the mouth to the count of 1-2-3-4-5-6. This is an easy process commonly known as the 3-3-6. You can increase it to 4-4-8 as you find your rhythm and it begins to feel unforced.

4-7-8 Breathing

Another highly recommended pattern is the 4-7-8:

- ~ Place your hands over your abdomen, drop your elbows, relax your shoulders and place the tip of your tongue on the roof of your mouth (tip touching tissue behind front teeth).
- ~ Empty your lungs exhaling through your mouth (because of the position of your tongue you make a whooshing sound).
- ~ Close your mouth and inhale through your nose to the count of 1-2-3-4.
- ~ Hold your breath to the count of 1-2-3-4-5-6-7.
- ~ Exhale through your mouth to the count of 1-2-3-4-5-6-7-8.
- ~ You can do up to 4 rounds at each sitting to begin with and gradually increase to a maximum of 7.

Pursed-Lip Breathing

This is another simple, effective technique which can be used to control your breath and calm you:

- ~ Breathe in slowly through the nostrils to the count of 1-2 (not deep, a normal breath).
- ~ Purse your lips (as if blowing out a candle) and breathe out slowly through your pursed lips to the count of 1-2-3-4.

Diaphragmatic Breathing

Diaphragmatic breathing is useful in the treatment of anxiety and hyperventilation. It involves breathing deeply into your lungs by flexing your diaphragm. When we breathe diaphragmatically, our stomach and abdomen expand rather than the chest. This is a modified version which, if used properly, will help you to relax. I found it to be especially useful when I was having sleep difficulty.

Lie on your back with knees bent and put your hand just below your rib cage. Then breathe in slowly, focusing on the breath and the feel of your hand as your stomach moves (out when inhaling and in when exhaling).

This can be done initially for 5-10 minutes about 4 times daily. It is also useful for whenever you feel anxious, have difficulty sleeping or feel a panic attack coming on. It can also be done sitting in a comfortable position. It is safe to gradually increase the time you spend doing it. Try to have a longer out-breath than in-breath. You can also breathe out with pursed lips through your mouth.

Emotional Freedom Techniques (EFT)

Emotional Freedom Techniques (EFT) is an acupressure technique which is often described as psychological acupuncture. It is easy to learn and is reported to be effective in the treatment of many conditions. It is widely recognised as an effective coping tool for anxiety-related issues and is found to be useful during withdrawal.

EFT involves tapping with the fingertips on special meridian points on the face, body, and hands, while repeating statements designed to provide release from the negative emotions. The creative use of the statements allows the person to tune in to the issue being addressed and when combined with the tapping, clears any related blockages or energy disruption. It is not necessary to understand how EFT works in order to benefit from it.

There are different variations of the technique but when I was challenged with serious withdrawal symptoms and found it hard to focus, I did a mini version which was still effective. (More information on EFT can be found in the Resources Guide.)

Exercise

Exercise is beneficial and conducive to wellness. If you are able to do any form of exercise during withdrawal you will fare better. If you have not had a regular exercise regimen and have decided to implement a routine to help you through withdrawal, please do so gradually and at a gentle pace as too vigorous exercise too quickly is also reported to exacerbate symptoms.

Even aerobic exercise which is known to be beneficial in reducing anxiety and depression can trigger adrenaline rushes that may worsen withdrawal symptoms. If you are finding that you react easily to stimuli, low impact exercise such as simple yoga asanas, light swimming or walking outdoors are other safe options.

It can be difficult to identify triggers because of the complexities of withdrawal and the many confounding factors. If you do notice a flare-up of symptoms, extreme lethargy or fatigue after commencing a new exercise regimen, it could mean that the additional stimulation is more than your nervous system can cope with at this time. Sticking to less strenuous exercise may then be your only option. Our bodies are brilliant at communicating and will always guide us.

Faith

The healing power of faith has long been discussed and studied and still remains controversial. The medical profession acknowledges that people who profess a faith in a higher power generally are better able to deal with illness and most Twelve-Step groups include faith as a source of support to their members. Conversely, to tell those who hold no particular belief to have faith will yield no results.

Quite often, the website receives emails from those who believe they would not have been able to have survived the depths of withdrawal without their faith. This is what has kept them sane, comforted and optimistic. Not only did I affirm during withdrawal, I also prayed fervently and felt deeply soothed and consoled as a result. Others have shared that the impact and intensity of withdrawal sent them straight back to the faith of their childhood or in search of spiritual sustenance.

One important aspect of faith which can be beneficial during withdrawal involves the use of prayer to acquire a deeply tranquil state. Repetitive prayer can produce a similar effect to the use of a mantra, or prayer words can be used in place of a mantra to reach a deep state of meditation. The use of prayer beads can also induce a meditative effect. The Roman Catholic rosary, the Hindu *japa mala,* Buddhist *juzu* or Muslim *mishbaha* have all been used in combination with repetitive prayer, with very positive effects.

The belief in and use of prayer is an amazing tool in providing hope and consolation during withdrawal. In addition, some people receive invaluable support from their faith-based groups and churches as they struggle to cope. If you believe in God, Source, Spirit, Buddha, Allah, Krishna - whatever your concept of a supreme force – you will be able to appreciate and relate to the reported power of faith. You may have found that it has helped you to cope better with your withdrawal. Faith is a lifeline for many.

Forums (Fora)

I vaguely recall joining a benzo forum some time in late 2003 or early 2004. I was so spaced out I don't remember exactly when, which forum, or what my user name was. After registering I never logged on because I could not relate to what I was reading. I think I read one or two posts and thought there was no way such misery could be my demise. I had no real understanding of benzo issues and the challenges people genuinely encounter. It was not until my second year of withdrawal that I wisely joined several forums and got some much needed support and validation.

I recall the suggestion once being made that the internet support for benzos is just mass hysteria and melodrama from people trying to sue their doctors or 'big pharma'. To the contrary, without the forums I do not know how the thousands of people who have no other support would cope - people whose doctors have no knowledge of tapering or withdrawal syndrome. In addition, the forums are where those in protracted withdrawal, who are at risk of being misdiagnosed find reassurance. Benzo users are fortunate to have them to turn to when guidance and additional support are needed.

It is also true that there are a lot of extremely worried, emotionally fragile, seemingly histrionic, mentally and physically traumatised people in 'benzo hell' who understandably post frantic messages. When they relate what they are experiencing this can have an impact on other members. There is no way of avoiding this as it is rare to find someone who has had a three-week, mildly unpleasant withdrawal joining a forum. This is why much of what is read can be disheartening.

If you are distraught and feeling vulnerable, do searches for your particular symptoms and try not to go through every single post absorbing other members' fear and anxiety related to symptoms you don't even have. Every forum has positive threads which give encouragement and reassurance. If you read something that has an uplifting effect and makes you feel hopeful, bookmark it and keep going back to it. Try not to focus on the symptoms and unfortunate accounts. Being supportive of other members can be rewarding too, leaving you distracted and less preoccupied with your own challenges.

Each forum is unique; one might be quite strict and nononsense and another more relaxed and feel-good. If you are a member of several you can use this to your advantage. When you are in a bad space emotionally you might frequent one of the more relaxed ones and if you need to be reined in you can visit a stricter one. It may also be wise to take a break from time to time, not just from the forums but anything benzo-related including this book, if you are finding it all too overwhelming.

Absorbing everything that can go wrong during withdrawal can make the process seem more daunting than it actually is. When you focus on positive forum messages that give useful coping tips, the quotes, music, books and movies that other members find uplifting, your withdrawal will be more tolerable. You may find that you end up having many good, light, pleasant days despite having to endure the symptoms. The most important thing during withdrawal is to look after yourself well and to be emotionally safe.

Grounding Tips

These are good, effective techniques which can be used to help you to feel grounded and more connected. They are particularly useful if you are experiencing feelings of anxiety, depersonalisation or derealisation.

- Feel your feet on the floor (take your shoes off if appropriate), and become aware of your bottom on the chair. Mentally note the sensation, the weight and the connection and stay with it for a while.
- Look around you. Notice the colour of the wall, are there any paintings, any plants in the room? If there is a clock, notice the time and then remind yourself of what day of the week it is and the date.
- Focus on your breathing and take deep slow breaths – in through your nose and out through your mouth.
- If you are outside, bring yourself to the present by becoming aware of the feel of the sun on your skin, or the rain if it's raining. If you can, lean against a tree. Inhale the scents of the grass and other plants. Listen to the sounds around you.

- Keep at least three items of different textures – something soft such as a stuffed toy, something smooth, rubbery, rough etc. As you hold them let the feel register and connect with them through your sense of touch.
- Imagine that your feet have roots that sink into the ground/earth. As you stand or sit, feel your feet making contact with the earth and deeply tune in to the connection. If appropriate and you are able to take your shoes off when you do this, it is even better.
- Stroke your cat or dog and say what you are doing while you do it. "I am stroking my cat..." Your pet may think your actions are strange but who else is capable of such unconditional acceptance?

Laughter Therapy

Laughter is therapeutic and healing. It releases endorphins which are the body's natural painkiller and promotes wellness. There is nothing like a good belly laugh to create a shift in energy. Some people have found that watching funny movies, video clips online and comedy re-runs on television can provide a distraction from the woes of withdrawal.

Yes, benzo withdrawal is a serious issue but humour helps. We learn to take ourselves and our circumstances less seriously. It does not mean discounting the experience or being flippant. It means that we have acknowledged that withdrawal is temporary and are incorporating every known positive pastime in an effort to make the experience as pleasant as possible.

Meditation

Meditating is another good way of coping with a withdrawal-induced hyperexcitable nervous system. Being able to learn a formal method of meditation can be challenging for those in intense withdrawal. They may not be able to sit up or maintain postures for prolonged periods due to the somatic effects such as extreme dizziness, muscle pain, shaking and involuntary movements. Or they may be having obsessive repetitive thoughts and are unable to focus. With tolerable symptoms, others are able to use meditation to derive welcome periods of restfulness.

When practising mindfulness meditation, the attention is usually focused on either the breath, a sound or mantra or imagery.

Here is a simple meditation:

Sit up in a comfortable position. Close your eyes. Breathe in and out through your nose. Concentrate on your breath noticing the air going in and air coming out. If your mind wanders, gently bring it back to the breath. It is that simple. You can do this for five minutes initially, gradually increasing the time as you become more comfortable with the practice. This can be expanded with the introduction of visualisation of a calming scene.

Unconscious Mind Exercise

Sit or lie in a relaxed position, take a few deep breaths or do a few rounds of your favourite breathing exercise, then say the following sentence out loud:

"Unconscious mind, I now allow you to do whatever you think is necessary in order for me to feel better."

This single sentence which I still use often, can be a most powerful, effective coping tool if applied accurately. It is the simplest yet most useful technique I have learnt to-date and it would be selfish of me to not pass it on. My big brother, who is a Neuro-Linguistic Programming (NLP) Master Practitioner, shared it with me when I was having very severe symptoms. He successfully uses this technique with clients and in his personal life. The first time I used it I was in a state of high-anxiety and had intense feelings of impending doom. I phoned him, did as instructed when I hung up, and immediately went to sleep. I woke up feeling more relaxed and refreshed than I had in months.

The unconscious or subconscious mind is a powerful healer. It is not external of us, will do us no harm and is the part of our psyche that knows best what we need at any given time. It is there to be accessed whenever we need it.

Falling asleep was my natural reaction, maybe because deep, rejuvenating sleep was what I needed at that time. However, the unconscious mind will deliver exactly what we request: whatever is necessary for us to feel better. It is our internal guidance system. You may find that without thinking, you pick up the phone and call someone who ends up giving you just the reassurance you need, or you suddenly gain a new perspective of your withdrawal which leads to full acceptance of the symptoms. I can only liken this exercise to having a total release of conscious control or achieving a form of complete surrender.

Visualisation

Visualisation involves focusing on an image of what you want and seeing it as already manifested. Although the imagination is used, visualisation is more profound than daydreaming or fantasising. It is a conscious use of one's will to see, in the mind's eye, desired scenes which can be of an event, a specific behaviour, or in the case of withdrawal, full recovery.

It is done in the first person and present tense. When doing visualisation, you can explore with all the senses. As you conjure up the image of yourself being fully recovered in your mind, what are you feeling, hearing, smelling and tasting? How is the scene unfolding?

The idea behind visualisation in withdrawal is that by directing and controlling the images in your mind, it can be used as a positive distraction to manage and cope with some symptoms. It is best to do a breathing exercise to relax prior to starting your visualisation exercise. Visualising yourself post-recovery is an excellent way to drift off to sleep or simply pass the time.

Work on Your Thoughts

Question any doubtful thoughts you may be having about your recovery. This approach is different to using affirmations or positive self-talk. For most in withdrawal, the two main culprits are: *I am never going to recover* and *something else must be wrong with me*. There is no way of knowing if either is true. Take a few moments to assess them, then work on them. Is this definitely, without uncertainty, going to happen? The answer is "No."

Yet, these thoughts which trigger a knee-jerk reaction are the source of worry and additional anxiety. They fuel so much fear that once entertained, a downward spiral begins leading to a most unfortunate sequence of events, culminating in a devastating (imagined) future. All of this anguish from a thought that is not true. How things may appear to you because of your current symptoms differs from the reality – which is that you will heal.

So, when thoughts of a permanent withdrawal or a dreaded disease creep into your mind, work on them. Ask yourself if they are absolutely true. Don't try to explain or justify them. Am I certain beyond doubt? Or, is there any possibility of another outcome? Yes, there is. The truth, what will serve you best right now, is that your symptoms are due to withdrawal and you are going to recover.

❧ 9 ❧

Stimulants,
Supplements & Diet

Not everyone discontinuing a benzodiazepine will find it necessary to monitor food, drink and supplement intake. Many are able to continue as usual. There are others, however, who are subject to a host of problems including gastrointestinal disturbances such as nausea, reflux, diarrhoea, constipation, stomach cramps and the infamous 'benzo belly' which causes distension.

With the gastrointestinal tract being sensitive to stress, it is no surprise that these issues surface. Furthermore, there are benzodiazepine receptors in this area. Although the function of these receptors has not yet been determined, it is thought that there is a link between their presence and the gastrointestinal withdrawal symptoms that some experience.

Supplements

There are conflicting reports regarding the taking of supplements during withdrawal. Some people report a noticeable negative reaction and others have found that some supplements seem to help. If you notice that you are sensitive to stimuli during withdrawal, it is best to be cautious and wait until recovery before taking supplements that may affect the nervous system. There really is no magic potion when it comes to recovery.

Magnesium, calcium, B vitamins, 5-HTP, taurine, melatonin, homeopathic remedies, GABA, valerian, kava – all these supplements may be beneficial in non-withdrawal situations but they cannot accelerate the repair of the GABA receptors. There is no evidence suggesting that they cause symptoms to disappear. If your withdrawal is not problematic then at best they will supply added nutrients. In terms of affecting the duration of withdrawal, anecdotal reports confirm that it can prolong the process in those who are sensitive. The use of supplements during withdrawal continues to be a highly debatable topic.

Taking supplements was ruled out in my case because I reacted every time. I had to be vigilant even in the later stages of recovery. I was not paranoid and it sometimes took a long time for me to identify the supplement in question as being the culprit. Months after my final wave, I tried transdermal magnesium to see if it would help to ease the residual spasms. I was confident about using supplements and did not anticipate being thrown back into a brief period of full withdrawal. I was horrified when I started having sweats, chills, shaking and intense vertigo. At first I thought: *Imagine having another wave so long after what I thought was my recovery,* but soon realised it was a reaction to the magnesium. I stopped using the magnesium spray and had no further recurrence of symptoms. My experience is not unique. Our website receives many emails from people who have reacted to supplements and this is the reason caution is recommended.

If you are already taking supplements and feel that they are making you feel better, there is no need to stop taking them. No flare-up of symptoms is a good indicator that it is okay to continue. If, however, you are having persistent symptoms, eliminating them may help to confirm whether or not they are complicating the withdrawal process and hindering your recovery. A hyperexcitable nervous system does not need additional stimulation.

Since withdrawal symptoms are due mainly to the down-regulation of our GABA receptors, then recovery is dependent on their repair and re-establishment of their affinity for the calming GABA. As far as I am aware, there is no supplement on the market known to accelerate this process. The most important thing during withdrawal is to feel as well as possible. Our bodies are so innately intelligent, they always find ways of communicating. All we have to do is listen.

Oral GABA

Of special note is oral GABA which some regard as the obvious cure. I bought GABA supplements when I was nearing the end of my clonazepam taper. It was part of my 'quick recovery' plan. It made sense that since long-term use of benzodiazepines affects the ability of the neural receptors to attract GABA, and this continues for some time after discontinuing the drug (because of damage to the receptors), then finding a GABA supplement would be a good substitute. Thankfully, before I took the supplements, I discovered that orally ingested GABA cannot be transported through the blood to the brain.

Furthermore, the post-benzo problems are not due to GABA deficiency but rather to the inefficiency of the damaged receptors in attracting the GABA that is already present. Even if the orally ingested GABA crossed the blood-brain barrier and we ended up having more than adequate GABA, our temporarily incapable receptors would not be able to attract it, and we would still end up with nervous systems in overdrive.

Alcohol

Alcohol is a central nervous system depressant which acts on the same GABA receptors in the brain as benzodiazepines. It affects the damaged receptors and interferes with the recovery process. If you are still taking a benzo then the combination can be dangerous, and in some cases, fatal. If you have already tapered but are still going through withdrawal, having even half a glass of alcohol is known to intensify symptoms.

Look out for hidden alcohol/ethanol in medicines including herbal tinctures and other preparations. Although this level of alcohol will be minuscule and under normal circumstances would have no effect, with a hypersensitive nervous system do not be surprised if you react. Withdrawal can do strange things to the body. I recall taking a cough mixture more than a year into my withdrawal; one dose caused a drastic reaction. My eyes got that old glassy look, I started having chills, shaking and sweating and could have been mistaken for a street drug addict in need of a fix.

As tempting as it may be, having alcohol during withdrawal is not worth the risk, especially if you are having troubling symptoms. It is advisable to avoid it at this time. The poor GABA receptors are already struggling to function and any interference in the process will be detrimental. Unless you eliminate it from your diet, you won't know if it is affecting your recovery. If you like relaxing with a good glass of wine, this is the perfect time to look forward to your recovery when you may once again be able to indulge.

Medication

There are contradictory reports from benzo users regarding their reaction to medication taken during withdrawal. Flu-like symptoms, gastrointestinal disturbances, joint and muscle pain are common at this time. Some people are able to take over-the-counter remedies without having adverse reactions; others report aggravated symptoms. These flare-ups tend to occur after the use of some types of antihistamines, opiate and codeine-containing painkillers, and flu remedies which include even minuscule amounts of alcohol/ethanol or caffeine.

Commonly prescribed antibiotics known as quinolones reportedly cause severe adverse reactions and should therefore be avoided. If you are prescribed this class of medication, please ask your doctor to find an alternative. It is good to remember too, that herbs also have pharmacological effects, some of which may exacerbate symptoms in susceptible individuals.

The best approach is to be observant. With brain fog and other cognitive problems, it is easy to unknowingly overlook simple precautions. Without becoming overly concerned or expectant, be quietly attentive to what you ingest. For those experiencing persistent and problematic symptoms, it is worth checking the labels and enclosed information leaflets.

There is no need to panic if you do react; simply stop taking that remedy and find a safer alternative. If you develop a viral infection or other condition that requires medication, it is better to take the recommended treatment and risk a flare-up of symptoms than suffer unnecessarily.

Dietary Modifications

Food is the one pleasure which some people feel they can explore and savour during withdrawal. Those individuals are able to eat normally. Others find that a simple diet works best for them at this time. Since gastric problems are so common, some users make the decision to modify their diets early on in their tapers. For those with food sensitivities and other troubling symptoms, nutritional balance is an ongoing quest. Any modifications that will make it easier on the digestive system can be used to one's advantage.

Caffeine is a stimulant which, if you are already hyperexcitable and are experiencing sleep difficulty, you may want to avoid or consume only early in the day. Those who are having a difficult withdrawal are advised to completely omit caffeine. If you are accustomed to having several cups of coffee or tea daily, it is best to gradually reduce your intake rather than suddenly abstain. Remember too, that decaffeinated beverages also contain a small but notable amount of caffeine.

Fluctuations in blood sugar is known to occur during withdrawal and some people report an exacerbation in symptoms when they consume sugary foods. Many people who use our website have reported that once they cut out or reduced their sugar intake, their symptoms lessened in intensity. This includes chemical sweeteners and ketchup. If you have a sweet tooth, stevia and yacon syrup are good and safe sugar substitutes. Yacon syrup is a natural, raw, low-calorie sweetener made from the root of the yacon plant. Stevia is another natural sweetener made from the leaf of the stevia plant. They both have negligible effects on blood glucose.

Other reported culprits during withdrawal are mono sodium glutamate (MSG), chocolates, which contain both caffeine and sugar, and very strong spices. Eliminating wheat is recommended if you are having to cope with constipation or benzo belly and watch out for processed ready meals which contain chemicals. It is not necessary to drink gallons of water as some do, but drinking adequate amounts is advisable.

Consuming small, frequent meals that contain foods with low glycaemic levels is believed to be of value to those with blood sugar fluctuations. Carbohydrates that break down slowly, releasing glucose gradually into the blood stream, have low glycaemic levels.

Highly glycaemic foods exacerbate hyperactivity (which we don't need).

This rough guide should give you an idea of the glycaemic index levels of some common foods:

Fruit

Apples, blackberries, blueberries, raspberries, cherries, grapefruit, kiwis, strawberries, oranges and pears are low. Bananas, mangoes, pineapples, red grapes, fruit cocktail and papayas are medium. Watermelons and dates are high.

Vegetables

Broccoli, alfalfa, cabbage, cauliflower, cucumber, watercress, spinach, tomatoes and brussel sprouts are low. Sweetcorn and beetroot are medium. Pumpkin, parsnips and swede are high.

Other

Almonds, brazil nuts and peanuts are low. With the exception of broad beans, most beans and pulses including lentils and chick peas are low. Fish, shellfish and lean, skinless meats are low. Pastas are low to medium, depending on type. Rices including brown rice are medium to high, depending on type.

Cornflakes, honey-coated, puffed and other processed cereals are high. Potatoes fried, baked and mashed are high. Doughnuts, muffins, white bread, commercial wheat bread and bagels are high.

Green Smoothies

We have already established that recovery from benzo withdrawal is dependent on our GABA receptors regaining their affinity for the calming GABA. As this process takes place, those with troubling gastric disturbances who have had to modify their diets and abstain from supplements may become concerned about nutritional deficiencies.

I discovered green smoothies post-recovery and wished I had been aware of them when I was struggling to cope and bordering on malnourishment. I have since shared them on the website and have received many good reports of improved energy and other benefits. This is not an endorsement of green smoothies as a benzo withdrawal cure. I do think that those with digestion issues, benzo belly and sensitivity to supplements may benefit though, as fruit and vegetables are usually well tolerated by most. Having a green smoothie or two daily will ensure that you're not missing out on a lot of vital nutrients.

Green smoothies as described by Victoria Boutenko in her book, *Green for Life*, are a good source of nutrients including amino acids. A bonus is that they take literally a few minutes and very little energy to make. During withdrawal I made fruit smoothies daily using low glycaemic fruit with natural bio yogurt. I also tried to have as many vegetables as possible. With this combination of fruit and vegetables it is easy to have your daily allowance in one go. Since having these drinks, I have noticed that my nails and hair have a new sheen, my eyes are clearer, my vision has improved and I no longer need my glasses to use the computer; my energy levels are high, I have no cravings and feel rejuvenated.

Kale is high in vitamins C and K and beta carotene and it is also one of the richest vegetable sources of calcium, iron, magnesium, manganese, potassium and phytochemicals. Spinach is a rich source of vitamins A, K, C, E, B2 and B6, copper, protein, phosphorous and zinc. In addition, it is a good, natural source of omega-3 fatty acids, niacin and selenium.

Here are a few delicious recipes. Some people use just one banana with half an avocado for creaminess and add stevia or yacon syrup to make them sweeter.

1-2 mangoes
2-3 handsful of baby spinach or kale
1 cup water

1-2 bananas
1/2 cup raspberries
1 pear
2 handsful baby spinach or kale
1 cup water

1-2 bananas
2 oranges
2 handsful of baby spinach or kale
(With oranges no water is necessary.)

1 -2 oranges
1-2 bananas
4-5 strawberries
½ head romaine lettuce

Notes:

Raw kale and cabbage should be used with caution by anyone with an under-active thyroid as they are what is termed 'goitrogenous' and interfere with iodine uptake. Also, because kale has a very high concentration of vitamin K, people on anti-coagulants (blood thinners) should consider this property as the drug attempts to lower vitamin K.

Even organic fruit and vegetables should be washed thoroughly so be sure to give them a thorough wash.

In order to get your nutrients, the most important thing is to add at least two large portions of fresh, green leafy vegetables to whatever fruit you choose to use.

Caution:

If you are aware or suspect that you react negatively to a certain fruit or vegetable, please do not add it to your smoothie.

You will need to chew the mixture and swallow slowly as if having a regular meal. Drinking them too quickly will shock your digestive tract and cause stomach upset.

During the first few days of drinking these smoothies some people experience what is referred to as 'green smoothie detox'. They may feel nauseated or have mild headaches. If you are experiencing troubling symptoms, the last thing you need is to have to deal with additional problems. Please consider waiting until you are well enough before trying green smoothies.

Moderation, being vigilant without becoming paranoid, and observing the way our bodies respond to stimuli of any kind is the best approach during withdrawal.

❧10❧

Giving Support to
Someone in Withdrawal

Compassion fatigue or burnout occurs when a caregiver becomes emotionally, socially, mentally and sometimes physically exhausted, resulting in apathy or lack of ability, willingness or energy to provide further attention and care. This is a natural response to the upheaval associated with especially chronic or intense situations and benzodiazepine withdrawal is no exception.

It can be difficult for family, friends, doctors and other caregivers to fully understand the effects of withdrawal. No amount of empathy can prepare them for the impact of the physical and psychological symptoms, personality changes and emotional challenges, as well as the practical support which may be required. It is not unusual for them to allude to an overreaction or to the medication causing some form of permanent mental or physical disorder.

Because of this, it requires unconditional acceptance to support someone going through withdrawal from benzodiazepines. This also includes those who are still on the medication and may be experiencing tolerance symptoms, as well as those who may take the drug erratically and are unknowingly experiencing interdose withdrawal. It is not only in the acute stages that support is needed.

If you care for someone who is withdrawing from a benzodiazepine and are experiencing some or all of the following, you may be at risk of becoming burnt out.

- feeling tired, drained and lethargic
- feeling overwhelmed and helpless
- having frequent headaches and other minor physical complaints
- feeling constantly worried
- feeling agitated or easily irritated
- feeling sad and hopeless
- overeating or loss of appetite
- sleep difficulty or oversleeping
- loss of interest in activities previously enjoyed

Tips

These tips, if adhered to, will help you to cope better, provide the required support and not become fatigued.

- Learn more about withdrawal and what it entails: The more knowledgeable you are about benzodiazepines and withdrawal, the better prepared you will be to cope with its stages and idiosyncrasies. You will find that you are more understanding and accepting of the person's experience and will be well equipped to give the support needed.
- Give unconditionally: You may have your own ideas regarding how withdrawal should be dealt with and what coping strategies and treatment are appropriate. As much as you may be able to empathise, you will not know what the person is going through. Resist suggesting visits to psy-

chiatrists, accelerating or slowing tapers, reinstating the drug, querying other diagnoses such as chronic fatigue syndrome (CFS), multiple sclerosis (MS), lupus, irritable bowel syndrome (IBS) or a mental breakdown and allow the time and space required to heal. Leave it up to him or her to direct you and say what is needed.

- Withhold judgement: The true effects of benzodiazepines are understated and many people find it difficult to accept that taking a legally prescribed drug could result in such adverse reactions. Try to be open and not make judgements based on assumptions or what you perceive to be credible. Even many well-intentioned medics are unaware and un-educated about the full repercussions of long-term benzo-diazepine use, specifically dependency and withdrawal.

- Release expectations: Appreciate that you have no control over the recovery process so that you don't feel responsible or pressured. The benzodiazepine withdrawal experience is unique and unpredictable; you may have to provide support for a much longer period than anticipated.

- Give practical support: The person you are caring for may be in severe discomfort and feeling extremely lethargic and depleted of energy. Mowing the lawn, cooking, cleaning, shopping and attending to the children can seem like in-surmountable tasks during withdrawal. (Parents with young children can have an exceptionally difficult time cop-ing with demands.) Also, for those with intense symptoms, any form of exertion can cause flare-ups. Offering to help with practical matters will make a positive difference.

- Listen actively: Withdrawal can be overwhelming and the person may be feeling traumatised. Talking is therapeutic and some people feel a need to talk about their experience. Follow his or her cues: if you can, listen actively - without judgement or preconception - as feelings and concerns are shared; at other times space or companionable silence may be all that is needed. Remember too, that non-verbal communication can be powerful and your warmth, acceptance, expressions and body language are even more important than your words.

- Don't take things personally: If the person you are caring for is agitated or becomes angry and overly-sensitive, try not to take it personally. The effects of withdrawal can cause mood swings, organic fear, paranoia and a host of other psychological symptoms. Understanding that these reactions are normal will allow you to accept them for what they are while you continue to give your support.

- Look after yourself well: Eat healthily, exercise regularly, maintain your hobbies, and get the rest and relaxation you need. Set limits and commit to what is realistic, rather than feel obligated to deliver on promises you are unable to keep as this will drain you even more. If possible, arrange a respite or back-up person who is reliable and trustworthy so that you can take regular breaks.

- Get emotional support: Caring for someone in withdrawal can be mentally draining so you need to ensure that you take care of your own emotional needs and receive adequate support at this time. It is also important that you have a trusted friend or relative to discuss your fears, needs and feelings with. If you become emotionally drained and fatigued you will have nothing left to give.

- Reassure, reassure, reassure: More than anything, someone experiencing withdrawal needs reassurance. Persistent, intense symptoms can cause doubt and increased anxiety. You will need to keep encouraging and reassuring your loved one that recovery is taking place. Hope is one of the most valuable coping tools and your attitude can make a big difference.

- Keep in touch: Keep in contact even when it seems the person has recovered. Withdrawal symptoms often come in 'waves' and you may mistake a period during which the symptoms temporarily subside to be full recovery. Many people are devastated when the symptoms resurface and this is when you may be needed the most.

∞11∞

Suicidal Ideation

Suicide is still a taboo subject with much associated ignorance and stigma. This often results in the reluctance of many who feel suicidal to seek assistance. The fear of being regarded as 'crazy' can make a person in crisis not reach out for help. Even in cases where allusions to having suicidal ideation are made: *I wish I could go to sleep and never wake up*, people may hesitate to ask if suicidal thoughts are present out of concern that they are 'putting ideas' in the person's head. This is not the case. Asking the question is a good way of giving permission to talk and makes it easier for those at risk to share their feelings.

Benzo withdrawal brings with it many physical and emotional challenges which can lead to prolonged low moods. It is understandable that having unrelenting symptom after symptom can be difficult and often makes recovery seem less than a remote possibility. It is important to remember that withdrawal is indeed temporary in most cases and despite the symptoms, recovery is taking place. However, if a person is already feeling suicidal hearing this may not help to alleviate the depressive moods and feelings of hopelessness.

Unwanted thoughts

In addition, having unwanted repetitive, intrusive thoughts including those of taking one's life is reported to occur during withdrawal. These are either directly or indirectly due to the abnormal reaction caused by the temporary damage to the GABA receptors as a result of long-term use of the drug.

If you acknowledge the thoughts as being withdrawal-related and give yourself time by not acting on any impulses you may be experiencing, they will eventually pass. In the meantime, speaking to someone who is trained to listen actively as often as you need to, will make coping easier.

Resources versus ability to cope

Regardless of the reasons for having suicidal ideation, the reality is that the emotional and possibly physical pain associated with the benzo experience will have exceeded the resources available. This perceived inability to cope results in a desperate wish to find another way out. Many people give warning signs hoping that someone will care enough to notice and offer help. It does not mean they are mentally ill or weak in any way. They simply feel that they can no longer cope; not even that they want to die, just that they don't believe they have the strength and resources they need to be able to continue. They want to stop their emotional pain.

Help is available

If, for whatever reason, you are feeling that you can no longer cope with your situation, there is another way. If you are isolated with no friends or family around, there are people who genuinely care and want to help. Please don't burden yourself by trying to cope with this challenge alone. Help is only a phone call away.

You do not need to act on your impulses right away. A thought is a thought and nothing more; it does not have to lead to action. Talking with someone who will not judge you and is experienced in dealing with crises such as yours will help and you will feel the pressure being relieved. Please consider speaking to a friend or family member or contact an emergency helpline. (See Resources at back of book.)

What to Do If
Someone You Know Feels Suicidal

If you are reading this because a friend or family member has expressed an urge to end his or her life you could:

- Find out if the person has a plan in terms of what will be used (pills etc.), a set time and where.
- Make a safety contract with the person: one in which s/he promises to stay safe and not act on any thoughts until a certain time (usually until someone is able to be physically present); that he or she will contact a trained mental health professional, a doctor or hospital if the thoughts and urge persist. Even a promise to phone a designated family member or friend for immediate help is better than having the person on his or her own. Ideally you would stay with the person either on the phone or in person until help arrives.
- Not argue, judge or try to talk the person out of it. She or he is consumed with pain and is feeling emotionally overwhelmed and helpless. This is a time to listen without judgement and to be supportive. Listen for as long as is needed and allow the person to talk, cry, say nothing, vent... whatever it takes. Talking will bring relief from loneliness, release pent up feelings and cause a reduction in agitation.
- Don't allow the person to swear you to secrecy. There is a reason that mental health professionals exclude 'harm to self or others' from confidentiality clauses. Your friend or

family member may be angry with you but at least s/he will be alive.

- Form a 24-hour suicide watch. This can be done discreetly if necessary, by having family members or friends (who are grounded and capable) take turns to be present throughout the day and night.
- Remove all known means of carrying out the act including car keys, razor blades, knives, firearms, pills etc. from easy access.
- Encourage him or her to speak to a helpline worker.

Examples of distorted thoughts associated with suicidal ideation:

~ *I can't see my way out.*
~ *I can't make the sadness go away.*
~ *I can't see a future without pain.*
~ *I can't cope anymore.*

Open-ended questions

If you are concerned about someone who you feel may be having suicidal thoughts, there are ways of conversing that can lead the person to talking through the problem. This is a gentler approach than asking direct questions which may cause the person to become defensive or retreat. Furthermore, not every hunch will be accurate and there are times when a person will be in despair or overwhelmed and not have even the remotest suicidal thought.

An open-ended question as shown below rather than a closed-ended, yes/no question such as "Are you feeling suicidal?" facilitates exploration of feelings. As the person expresses, there is a reduction in agitation. This allows at least some concerns to be processed often to a point of emotional safety. A distressed person can sometimes be in conflict or at odds with his or her thoughts and feelings. These types of questions are non-confrontational and give more scope.

Examples of open-ended questions:

~ *"Can you tell me what you mean by that?"*
~ *"How did you feel when that happened?"*
~ *"When did you realise it was affecting you so badly?"*
~ *"What would be another option for you?"*
~ *"What do you think would happen if you did that?"*

'Attention-seeking' myth

If someone hints at wanting to commit suicide, please do not judge or make any assumptions. Discounting the importance of what has been shared with you by thinking the person is being melodramatic is not useful. Even if you conclude that the person is 'attention-seeking', please still go ahead and give the attention needed. It is better to be supportive and not have regrets.

I once pleaded with someone to get help for her teenage son whom I sensed was at high suicide risk; unfortunately, he was instead reprimanded for wanting attention. A few months later he took his life. I feel strongly about this issue. You will never truly know what is going on with another's emotions. When a person mentions suicide it is usually because urgent attention is needed. It is always wise to take him or her seriously and offer support.

Here are some of the criteria used to identify suicidal risk:

- Recurrent thoughts of or preoccupation with death.
- Recurrent or ongoing suicidal ideation without any plans, or ongoing suicidal ideation with a specific plan.
- Recent suicide attempt, history of depression or history of suicide attempts that required intervention.

- Positive family history of depression and/or a preoccupation with suicidal thoughts.
- Self-destruction or dangerous behaviour (such as reckless driving etc.) which appears to invite death.
- Self-inflicted injuries such as burns and cuts.
- Indirect statements such as "I can't go on much longer" or "This voice in my head wants me to do something crazy."
- Giving away possessions.

Debriefing

Exposure to this kind of situation can be emotionally taxing for the person handling the crisis. It is therefore advisable to have some form of debriefing. This will help to avoid vicarious trauma and other effects such as negatively judging the way the incident was handled. In an informal setting, one way of doing this can be to telephone a crisis helpline and speak to a worker. Without disclosing personal information, you can say what you did, share what you wished you had or had not said, how you felt you did and how you are feeling at the time of the conversation. This is not done for feedback but simply to help you deal with any difficult, residual feelings or uncomfortable emotions that may have arisen.

Finding someone to talk to who, without judgement, can facilitate the honest and frank exploration of difficult feelings, will provide immediate relief from distress. If, for whatever reason, you are experiencing suicidal ideation, please seek help. Conversely, if you suspect that someone is having thoughts of taking his or her life, please consider offering help.

∽12∽

Counsellors

A counsellor who is not fully aware of the complexities of benzodiazepine withdrawal syndrome will not be able to appropriately treat a client who is withdrawing from the drug. Unless the therapist understands that the client's psychological symptoms are mainly due to withdrawal, it is unlikely that any therapeutic approach or treatment plan will be effective. Attempting to treat a benzo user with only basic knowledge of chemical dependency results in misdiagnoses and causes additional trauma. Judging from the volume of emails received from concerned users whose therapists have alluded to their having serious mental health disorders, this is unfortunately still a common occurrence.

Consulting a therapist who is knowledgeable about benzodiazepine withdrawal will, on the other hand, empower and facilitate coping, reduce distress and increase the chances of a more manageable withdrawal.

Counselling During Withdrawal

There were times during withdrawal when I wished I had a benzo-wise counsellor to consult. I knew from my own training background that there was limited content on benzodiazepines in even the chemical dependency modules of most counselling training programmes. The focus was mainly on alcohol, nicotine and illegal drugs. I was therefore reluctant to consult any professional who was not aware of the full dynamics of benzodiazepine withdrawal syndrome.

When my neurologist ruled out withdrawal as the cause of the involuntary movements or drug-induced dyskinesia, apart from medication, I was offered cognitive behavioural therapy (CBT). I was first referred to the neuropsychiatry department of the hospital where I underwent a lengthy mental status examination. The neuropsychiatrist concluded that I had handled my withdrawal sensibly and was coping well. She felt that therapy would not help and seemed puzzled that I had been referred to her in the first place.

Despite her observations, a few weeks later I received an information package in preparation for my 'proposed six-week inpatient stay' at the hospital's psychiatric wing. I was deeply perturbed and quickly telephoned an ex-colleague and dear friend who is an experienced and brilliant psychotherapist. I pleaded with her to honestly tell me if she had concerns regarding any aspect of my behaviour. She had been checking on me frequently throughout my post-acute withdrawal period and had witnessed most of the symptoms. Like the neuropsychiatrist, she felt I was very much in awareness of the processes taking place and was coping exceptionally well. We agreed that it would be detrimental to my recovery to be admitted to the hospital. I wrote as gracious a letter as I could muster, thanking them for the care I was given. I then avoided further consultations until my symptoms abated.

My concern was whether or not the mental health professionals would have acknowledged my symptoms as being due to withdrawal and consequently, would I be treated with medication that would exacerbate my problems, hinder recovery or create further dependency issues. Having since communicated with thousands of other benzo users through our website, I am tempted to hug myself for my adamance. When I hear of their experiences with cocktails of medicines many of them were prescribed, I know I made the right decision.

The immediate need for a client in withdrawal is to relate the experience to a non-judgemental listener with the objective of finding ways of coping. A well-meaning counsellor who is not knowledgeable about benzodiazepines will inevitably identify reasons other than withdrawal for the psychological symptoms. This is only due to a lack of awareness and training and is not intentional. Still, it does not help that the client who is struggling to cope with the immediacy of the withdrawal effects may then be asked to explore childhood or relationship issues. This probing therapy can be overwhelming and emotionally damaging to someone who is neurologically over-stimulated, emotionally fragile and vulnerable.

In addition, emotional anaesthesia, the inability to feel pleasure or pain, is a common effect of chronic benzo use. This makes processing and exploration of feelings futile. If a person is unable to access authentic feelings due to the drug's effect, what is there to be processed? It is this point in question that renders counselling (by a therapist who is not knowledgeable about benzos) during withdrawal inappropriate in many cases. Furthermore, with withdrawal-induced brain fog, dysphoria, depersonalisation and derealisation, being misunderstood and misinterpreted could cause the client to become frustrated and severely depressed.

What Every Counsellor Should Know

To treat a current or ex-user of benzodiazepines without first acquiring in-depth knowledge of the drug and withdrawal syndrome can result in unintentional harm. A good understanding of benzo-related issues, not just general drug use, is essential.

The effects of long-term benzo use and resultant damage to the GABA receptors in the brain can cause temporary emotional and cognitive disruption which manifests in the most bizarre ways. Depersonalisation, derealisation, organic fear, feelings of impending doom, extremely high anxiety, paranoid ideation, repetitive thoughts, weepiness, emotional bluntness, mood swings and brain fog are just some of the common psychological problems which may be experienced during withdrawal. These symptoms do not only surface in clients with pre-existing anxiety or other psychological challenges. Many who were prescribed benzos for medical conditions also experience them. They are temporary, however, and usually disappear with recovery.

When assessing a client in the throes of withdrawal, you may note that many of the symptomatological criteria listed in the *Diagnostic and Statistical Manual of Mental Disorders (DSM IV)* are fulfilled. A nervous system in overdrive and a constant state of hyperexcitability can result in the most peculiar and unexpected psychological symptoms. This makes misdiagnosing a high probability and knowledge of benzodiazepines a necessity. If the symptoms surfaced during withdrawal, it is best to consider them as physiological and not due to a mental health issue. After the client has achieved full recovery and all the withdrawal symptoms have abated, further assessments of any remaining psychological issues may lead to a more accurate diagnosis and appropriate treatment.

In addition, memory impairment, confusion and lack of concentration are common both in current and ex-benzo users. Therapeutic treatment which involves maintaining a train of thought is ineffective; it can also be mentally and emotionally draining for these clients. It is only when the nervous system recovers and cognition improves that exploration and processing will work.

A client may have had deep emotional problems which are not related to benzos or withdrawal. They could have been the reason for which the drug was first prescribed. With discontinuance, these issues may resurface. Because of the complexities of long-term benzo use and withdrawal, it will be impossible to determine what is benzo-related and what is not. Again, it is in the best interest of the client to wait until post-recovery when the symptoms have subsided to address the pre-existing issues.

Anyone in benzo withdrawal will benefit most from active listening, constant reassurance, and empowerment through the learning of coping skills. Probing and processing of deep emotional problems should be postponed until after the repair of the damage caused by the drug. This will be achieved in due course and normal brain function will return. The ex-user will recover and any psychological symptoms caused by benzodiazepine withdrawal syndrome will disappear. Should there be any post-traumatic issues or return of an underlying psychological problem post-recovery, then an appropriate counselling or psychotherapeutic approach will certainly be beneficial.

∞13∞

Doctors

What Patients Wish Their Doctors Knew

While many doctors are aware of the dependency and withdrawal issues related to the long-term use of benzodiazepines, others are still limited in their knowledge and may consequently give substandard care, often putting their patients' safety at risk. The following are useful points which users wish their doctors were aware of at the times they were treated.

Symptoms

When taken long-term (more than four weeks), the patient can become dependent on the drug and may experience withdrawal symptoms when it is discontinued. This withdrawal experience is unique and symptoms vary according to individual. Common physical symptoms include: profuse sweating, headaches, nausea, dizziness, gastric disturbances, palpitations, chills, muscle pain, twitches, spasms and tremors. Psychological symptoms such as feelings of depersonalisation, derealisation, anxiety, panic attacks, cognitive 'fog' and distorted visual, tactile, auditory and gustatory perception are also common.

There are doctors who are aware of this and are able to reassure their patients that the symptoms are indeed withdrawal-related and will disappear once withdrawal is over. Sadly, this is not always the case and many patients with no pre-existing psychological problems end up being misdiagnosed and treated for schizophrenia, bipolar and other mental health disorders.

Cold Turkey

A patient should never be advised to discontinue taking a benzodiazepine abruptly. "Then stop taking it," was the reply of a well-intentioned doctor when I expressed my concern that the drug had lost its efficacy. It is surprising that many doctors still give this advice and our website often receives frantic emails from people experiencing extremely distressing symptoms as a result. Fortunately, I found information online which recommended a slow taper using diazepam (because of its longer elimination half-life) and was able to successfully wean off. Quitting cold turkey is dangerous and can cause serious problems including seizures and psychosis.

Tapering

The decision to withdraw should be the patient's and she or he must be allowed to taper off the drug at a comfortable pace using the most appropriate weaning process. The more common methods are: substituting with diazepam, titration by crushing the tablet into a powder and mixing it with water, and the direct method where the dosage is very slowly reduced. Factors to be considered include personal circumstances, overall general health, the stressors in the patient's life, stamina, support available and previous experience with drugs. It is most important that the patient feels in control of the process. Apart from the usual withdrawal challenges, being pressured into tapering too quickly can cause additional anxiety and hinder recovery.

Duration

The conflicting reports regarding the duration of withdrawal and whether or not protracted withdrawal exists poses one of the biggest problems for patients. Many website users are baffled when their doctors explain that since the drug has already left the body, it is impossible for them to still be experiencing withdrawal. This is inaccurate and misleading. When the benzodiazepine sub-units have been down-regulated, the process of re-synthesising and re-externalising onto the receptor assembly can take weeks, months or longer.

Doctors who are unaware of this usually acknowledge the acute and early post-acute stages of withdrawal. However, once symptoms persist longer, these patients are told the withdrawal period has ended and the problems are 'all in the head'.

Furthermore, as alternative diagnoses are queried, additional emotional energy is expended awaiting diagnostic tests results which are usually negative. When every test is exhausted, again, the suggestion that the problems are psychological and have nothing to do with withdrawal is inevitably made. This does not augur well for the unfortunate patients who then become concerned about the implied possibility of mental health issues, only to find that the symptoms disappear once the protracted period ends.

Benzo-wise doctors will agree that while many people recover within a six to eighteen-month period, it is not uncommon for a percentage of patients to experience symptoms (often interspersed with windows of normality) for two to three years or longer in rare cases.

'Pre-existing anxiety' myth

Because many patients are prescribed benzodiazepines for anxiety-related issues, the consensus is usually that the post-withdrawal syndrome or any protracted symptoms are in fact due to a resurgence of the pre-existing anxiety.

I was prescribed a benzodiazepine for a neuromuscular condition and had no history of anxiety, depression or any other psychological problem. The anxiety I experienced especially during acute withdrawal was inconceivable. I have also communicated with others who were prescribed benzos for medical problems and experienced intense organic fear and numerous anxiety-related symptoms. Pre-existing anxiety or not, a nervous system in a hyperexcitable state due to the down-regulation of GABA receptors can reduce the most grounded and stable person to literally a 'quivering wreck'.

It is the responsibility of every doctor who prescribes a benzodiazepine to give the patient information on which the decision to take or not take the drug can be based. When treating patients for anxiety, insomnia or other related conditions, a doctor might understandably be hesitant and conclude that imparting too much information will only make matters worse. However, keeping patients ignorant of the addictive properties of a drug is not in their best interest; this is the reason for the 'unpleasant surprise factor' that presents in the form of withdrawal.

The *Ashton Manual - Benzodiazepines: How They Work & How To Withdraw* should be compulsory reading for every healthcare professional. It has additional information on symptoms, tapering schedules, equivalence tables, Z drugs which are similar to benzos, effects of other medication such as quinolones, and everything required to ensure that a patient withdrawing from a benzodiazepine is given the best possible care.

Tips on Dealing With Doctors

Due to the complexities of withdrawal and the many baffling symptoms that often present, you may not be able to avoid visits to your doctor to rule out other probable causes. While there are many brilliant, dedicated doctors whose main concern is their patients' welfare, unfortunately, very few are aware of issues related to benzodiazepine use. If you end up having to consult your doctor during withdrawal, here are a few tips I have gleaned from my experience which might come in handy. Although you may detect what I hope is considered a humorous undertone, this is important information which should be taken seriously. It will help to reduce the risk of your being misdiagnosed.

- Don't be too subdued; this will be noted as your being 'depressed' or 'of flat affect'. Although your current state is due to withdrawal, it is likely that your well-intentioned doctor may not be aware of this.
- Don't be too animated or expressive; this will be mistaken for your being 'agitated', 'volatile' or 'manic'.
- Don't understate your symptoms; you need to give your doctor enough information to properly assess your condition. Plus the conclusion may be made that nothing is wrong with you.
- Don't overstate your symptoms; you will appear to be 'neurotic' or 'irrational'.
- Don't be too long-winded. Time per consultation is limited and you may be tuned out after the fourth sentence. State the most important facts first and quickly, before the doctor gets that glazed look and reaches for the prescription or referral (to the psychiatrist) pad.
- Don't dress shabbily; it will be deemed inappropriate and what you say will be given less credence.
- Don't over-dress; it will be deemed inappropriate and what you say will be given less credence.

- Don't use too many medical terms or appear to be knowledgeable about benzos and withdrawal. Whatever you do, make sure you say "pee" and not "micturate," or "my heart was beating fast," not "I was tachycardic." Even if you normally use these terms, try not to on this occasion. If you do, your doctor will think you have been watching too much *ER, Grey's Anatomy* or *Holby City*.

- Don't self-diagnose; even if you are 99.9% certain your symptoms are withdrawal-related, resist the urge. Instead, casually state that they could be as a result of withdrawal and give the doctor a copy of the section of the *Ashton Manual* that lists the symptoms. It is regarded as a credible authority on benzodiazepines and your doctor should be impressed.

- And most importantly, do not be surprised if your doctor tells you that your symptoms cannot be due to benzo withdrawal. I eventually stopped mentioning the 'w' word after being consistently told it could not possibly last so long.

If a symptom is causing concern or serious discomfort it is best to seek medical attention.

∞14∞

Employment and Debt

Employment

The stress of having to work during withdrawal can worsen symptoms. Some people with mild and tolerable symptoms are able to continue working. Others are too ill to do so and are house bound. An unfortunate percentage who are the sole earners in their families are challenged with the struggle of working throughout the recovery process. These are some of the ways in which withdrawal can affect work:

- increased periods of absenteeism and sick leave
- impaired performance and productivity
- poor time-keeping
- tendency to lose concentration
- tendency to become confused
- memory impairment
- mood swings, irritability or aggression
- low energy or lethargy
- deterioration in relationships with management
- deterioration in relationship with colleagues
- deterioration in relationships with clients
- risks of accidents with jobs which involve driving, the use of machinery or dangerous equipment

Many people in withdrawal are faced with the dilemma of whether or not they should mention the prescribed drug dependency and if yes, how much do they then disclose. Do they risk the possibility of having to deal with the stigmas attached to tranquilliser use and explain about benzodiazepines and withdrawal? Do they accept other diagnoses such as generalised anxiety disorder or depression in order to obtain approved sick leave? Those with troubling physical symptoms which mimic conditions such as irritable bowel and chronic fatigue syndromes may tend to prefer a medical rather than psychological diagnosis. I am aware of cases where patients accept any misdiagnosis and will not argue with their doctors when told the symptoms can no longer be regarded as benzo-related, in order to get time off from work.

How a withdrawal-related work issue is managed is often determined by the employer-employee relationship and the organisation's health and safety policies. Those who are unable to take time off from work will benefit from having an understanding employer who will allow flexibility in work conditions. Having the minimum number of stressors at this time is the most important factor and coping with a troubling withdrawal could necessitate extended sick leave, reduction in work hours, or a transfer to a less demanding post. Bearing in mind that withdrawal does not normally last indefinitely, any action taken will be temporary. Once you are recovered, you will be able to resume work. Having overcome this challenge, you may even end up feeling confident and inspired enough to embark upon a new career.

Ultimately, successfully coping with withdrawal and achieving recovery should be priority. Having an income is important but if working interferes with your recovery process, you will need to assess the advantages to determine whether or not they are worth the resultant hindrances.

Debt

One of the often overlooked repercussions of having a long, protracted withdrawal is financial difficulty. Apart from being disabling, a troubling withdrawal can cause vulnerability to debt problems. As we are already aware, a combination of physically and psychologically impairing symptoms can cause an inability to work or a reduction in work hours for some. There are many cases of people who, at the unexpected onset of acute withdrawal, are thrown into a period of personal crisis without the capacity to attend to their financial concerns. This causes a rapid accumulation of debt problems and the person can be so unwell and cognitively impaired that she or he is unaware or unable to seek advice or claim state benefits.

Harassment from unsympathetic creditors, job loss, inability to pay the mortgage and fear of losing one's home are just a few of the additional financial issues that can present with withdrawal and contribute to higher levels of anxiety.

As we know, although temporary, benzodiazepine withdrawal can persist for much longer than anticipated. In many cases, being granted state benefits specifically for 'benzodiazepine withdrawal' can be difficult and in this situation, settling for an anxiety-related diagnosis may be regarded as an acceptable alternative.

If you are experiencing financial difficulties as a result of benzo withdrawal, you are entitled to assistance in the form of advice and benefits. Your claim is legitimate and should be regarded as no different to those of patients with other disabilities.

Should you be concerned about stigmatisation or prejudicial judgements in the case of advice regarding your debt problems, you will need to weigh this against the toll that the stress of being in debt will take on your health. Your recovery should take precedence over every other issue.

With regard to state benefits, your first few claims may be declined and you may have to re-apply. Please do not let this deter you. Keep persisting and you will succeed. If you are incapable of completing the arduous process, there are voluntary organisations and agencies such as the Citizens Advice Bureau (United Kingdom) that will provide the necessary information, advice and assistance with applications.

❦ 15 ❦

Litigation

"**T**ell me you're suing that doctor, right?" I recall these to be the first words uttered by those who knew me in the pre-benzo days when they saw how unwell I was during withdrawal. The subject of litigation in regard to irresponsible prescribing of benzodiazepines can be controversial, but after receiving numerous queries via the website, I believe it is relevant and will share my experience.

Most people who have had a difficult time withdrawing from a benzodiazepine suffer significant losses. Apart from having to endure the troubling symptoms, the stigmas, misdiagnoses, loss of relationships and other traumas, there can be additional repercussions such as loss of income and property.

For varied reasons, they may consider taking legal action against their doctors. Some may be incensed that they were not warned of the drug's effects and were not given the option of making an informed decision. Others hope to make an example of their case, and some simply need compensation for their losses in order to effect a new beginning. I am also aware that fair compensation is the wish of many relatives and friends who witness the adverse effects and repercussions of benzo dependency.

Overview

Clinical negligence is the breach of a legal duty of care by a doctor or other healthcare professional and their employers.

With reference to the United Kingdom, it must be proven:

- That the doctor or other healthcare professional owed a duty to take care of the patient and not cause injury;
- That there was a breach of this duty and he or she failed to meet the relevant standards of a reasonable body of other doctors in that field;
- That this failure or breach of duty directly caused harm or significantly contributed to the patient's injuries;
- That this harm resulted in damage or losses such as a recognised psychiatric injury or disorder, financial loss, etc.

The limitation period for bringing legal proceedings for clinical negligence resulting in physical or psychiatric injury is three years from the date of the negligence, or from the date that the injured person becomes aware of it. At the discretion of the courts, this can be extended under certain circumstances including the claimant being deemed mentally incapable.

My Litigation Experience

During my second window of clarity, I reflected on the nightmare I had been through (thinking it was over) and firmly decided I was going to sue the initial prescribing doctor for not warning me. I knew that there was no way that I, a grounded, emotionally balanced woman with no history of psychological problems would ever have taken even half of one of those 'pills' had I been told of the dependency issues. I was traumatised, shell-shocked and felt compelled to do something about it.

I was fortunate to have had access to the expertise of my father who is a barrister and was still practising at the time. He was called to the bar at Middle Temple in London in the mid 1950s and is highly regarded as a veteran lawyer in the Caribbean region where he resides.

As soon as I shared my plans, he discouraged me. On a personal note, he felt it would be too drawn-out and emotionally taxing a process without his being present to support me. I was living on my own and was quite isolated. He also immediately identified that my having had the pre-existing eye tic would create a problem in proving causation with regard to the current involuntary movements. I was adamant though, so I threw a mini tantrum on the phone as daughters do, and proceeded to seek further advice.

Too unwell to focus

After an initial conversation with a solicitor who was empathetic and understanding, I was asked to research and collate information. I soon realised that I was much too unwell to even attempt to do what was required. The solicitor asked me to submit the names of all the doctors who had prescribed the drug, the names of all the other doctors who were a part of these practices at the time and the names of the National Health Service trusts. I also had to acquire copies of my notes to confirm the date I first discovered the *Ashton Manual* in order to establish the limitation period.

When I first spoke to this solicitor, I was experiencing a window of clarity and was quite lucid. However, the symptoms soon intensified. I could hardly sit up or construct a coherent sentence. Focusing long enough to make the phone calls to acquire the required information was an impossibility. I was also instructed to make a note of the names of the people I spoke to, the time and date. It was overwhelming. Before my application for legal aid was completed, I wrote to the solicitor stating that I had decided not to proceed.

Gag order

My greatest concern was receiving a 'gag order' which would restrict me from making any information or comments public. I would not be able to discuss my withdrawal experience or the case. I was already journalising my progress and had committed to promoting benzo awareness. There was no way I was going to 'be quiet', not even with a muzzle. I was therefore relieved when I made the decision to discontinue the case.

Legal aid approved

Fast forward to my next window of clarity a few months later. Again, after evaluating the impact of what had happened to me, I decided to go ahead with investigating the possibility of suing. I was clinging to the hope that I would make an example of my case and also receive the compensation I felt I needed to be able to start over. This time I was more coherent and my legal aid was approved. I exhaled, resolved to not be anticipatory or invest emotionally, and continued my writing.

As soon as the process began, I became concerned about the initial prescribing doctor who I genuinely felt was well-meaning. I don't know why, but I was worried that my claim would disrupt his life and career. That feeling soon dissipated, however, when the symptoms persisted and I continued to be so unwell I could do nothing but sit at home and scribble in my journals. This triggered renewed resolve and I felt that my case could make him and his colleagues at least a bit more cautious when prescribing benzodiazepines for long-term use.

Expert's Opinion: The Verdict

After more than a year and a half, my solicitor acquired all my notes, finalised my witness statement and sent them off to an expert for a report. This would determine whether or not the case would proceed as the expert's opinion weighs heavily on the decision the Legal Services Commission makes as to whether or not to continue funding a case.

When I saw the report I was shocked but could see how easy it was for both my statement and notes to be misinterpreted. I just did not have the mental capacity required at the time I gave my statement, and it was incomplete and ambiguous in places. Furthermore, I could hardly recognise myself from my notes which were filled with discrepancies.

It is too lengthy to include everything here but the report stated that:

1. The expert agreed that all my problems (apart from the pre-existing tic) were clearly due to benzodiazepine withdrawal syndrome.

   At the risk of sounding absurd, I was relieved to have read this and felt that despite already being one hundred percent certain that this was indeed the case, it was good to receive confirmation from an expert. This statement alone made the investigation of the claim worthwhile.

2. I should never have come off the drug in the first place as instructed by my doctors.

   This was a shock, especially since the drug was what had made me so unwell. Also, none of the doctors had ever advised me to stay on the drug. The fact was that none of the doctors who issued the seven plus years of repeat prescriptions ever discussed any aspect of my taking the clonazepam. If I had not found Professor Ashton's manual, chances are I would still be in a semi-comatose state on the medication.

3. The expert felt that my protracted withdrawal was due to my still taking diazepam 'as needed' and that I should cut out benzodiazepines altogether.

I was aghast when I read this until I re-read my witness statement in which I had told the solicitor that my only prescription was for diazepam to be taken as needed. This was true at the time because my doctor had prescribed diazepam at the end of my taper to be taken in the case of the involuntary movements becoming too frequent or intense. However, I never touched them and eventually threw them away.

4. The expert kept referring to my 'severe neurological disorder' which was getting worse.

I did not fully understand this since I wouldn't consider a tic to be severe. I imagine it has to do with my inaccurate notes and the many consultations and diagnostic tests performed during the tolerance years, before I discovered the drug was the source of my problems. I do not know how I could have had a 'severe neurological disorder' and still drive, exercise, dance etc. without needing medication, and for all those years? This one didn't make sense.

5. The prescription of clonazepam long-term would be justified on a risk/benefit analysis to control this severe deterioration of my neurological disorder.

Of course, if I had had a 'severely deteriorating neurological disorder' this would indeed have been this case.

6. Long-term prescription of clonazepam for movement disorders is approved in the *British National Formulary* (BNF) and the expert felt that my being prescribed the drug was justified.

Decision to drop the case

There was much more to my case. After reading the expert's report and seeing my medical notes which mentioned diagnoses I did not know I was supposed to have had and drugs I had never taken, I decided to drop the case. I had managed to remain emotionally detached during the entire process but was beginning to feel saddened and frustrated. Because of the three-year limitation issue, I was forced to prepare a witness statement long before I was mentally capable and just did not have the coherence, memory and other cognitive abilities to do it well at the time.

My solicitor was very professional and his interest in my case somehow made me feel secure. I felt as if my 'back was being watched' while I tried to reason with the medics who were recommending other treatment which would have exacerbated my symptoms. After receiving the expert's report, my solicitor felt that we could proceed on the grounds of 'lack of informed consent' but it would be fraught with difficulty, the costs would be enormous and the compensation insignificant. It was up to me to decide, but he could not confirm that further legal aid funding would be granted given the expert's conclusions. I knew that unless I won the lottery in order to self-fund the case, my chances of success were ruined.

During the entire process the solicitor and I met only once and this was during a fairly good window of clarity when the symptoms were bearable. I realised that I had not given him enough information when he stated in his final letter that some people use a razor blade to cut the tablets in the final stage of their taper and that he hopes that if I take the expert's advice and cut out benzos altogether, it will resolve the protracted symptoms. I recall crying and thinking, *But I too had to use a razor blade and tapered slowly, and I haven't taken a benzodiazepine since the end of my taper!* I felt misunderstood and was annoyed with myself for not having fully explained my circumstances. I later consoled myself that given my then limited faculties, I had done my best.

Letting go

I accept responsibility for the misinterpretation of my case; I had not told my initial prescribing doctor that I wanted to stop the tics for my wedding day. How could I when it seemed such a vain and superficial reason? Instead I told him I felt the tics were becoming distracting. He may have interpreted this to mean the tics were worsening, but it still doesn't justify the use of 'severe deterioration'.

In hindsight, the timing was wrong. I know that the coherent 'me' would have been a solicitor's ideal client. I even think that had I been fully lucid, I would have considered representing myself. Prior to this benzo experience that is something I would have attempted without hesitating.

I felt so strongly about being misunderstood and my case being misinterpreted, I wanted to write to the expert to clarify that I had not taken the medication since the end of my taper, that I did not have a severely deteriorating neurological problem and that like the other withdrawal symptoms, the spasms are improving and I know without a doubt that they will eventually go. My residual fitting had nothing to do with the worsening of a 'severe neurological disorder'. It was undoubtedly benzodiazepine withdrawal and I have connected with others who have had similar withdrawal reactions. I consider these involuntary movements to be drug-induced dyskinesia.

It took some time for me to come to terms with the outcome. I was happy that I had not invested in it emotionally and, apart from the devastation I felt when I read the expert's report and saw my notes, was not too perturbed. I have now been able to release and let this chapter go. For some reason, it was not meant to be and I have willingly accepted that. Who knows? A 'gag order' would have prevented me from sharing my story and contributing to benzo awareness - the most useful and rewarding things I have done in my life.

I would never discourage anyone from seeking compensation and I am aware that there are successful benzo cases, most of which have been settled out of court.

Factors to be Considered

- Any form of litigation can be soul-destroying and so you will need to maintain a degree of emotional detachment, especially if you are on your own and still in withdrawal as the associated stress may be detrimental to your recovery. Still, passion and determination are required. When I think of my own case, I can now see that I was definitely too detached from the process.
- Having your funding approved does not mean you will receive a settlement. That is only the beginning. These cases are complex and until an expert gives a favourable opinion, it is best to remain objective and not start your wish list.

Even with an expert's backing, there are other loopholes. So, without being negative, I would say it is best to wait.

- If you have pre-existing or concurrent medical or psychological conditions your case will be more complex so you will need to mentally prepare yourself for this. I had an eye tic which was deemed a mild neurological quirk and was surprised when it was described as a 'severely deteriorating neurological disorder'.

- Try to get copies of your notes early on in the process, ideally before you make your decision. They will trigger your memory (or not, if there are inaccuracies) and help you to determine at first glance, how your case may be viewed. Also, if pertinent information goes missing, you will already have had a copy.

- If you did not have a pre-existing psychological condition, were prescribed the drug for a medical condition and causation can be proven that your injury is psychological or medical (and not relating to the condition for which it was prescribed), your case may be more definable.

If you are still in the throes of withdrawal, you could consider waiting until you are well enough before initiating legal proceedings. As you may have gleaned from reading this, inability to recall relevant information because of cognitive impairment can adversely affect a case's outcome.

∞16∞

Recovery

Recovery from withdrawal can be like a rebirth. Imagine that you have experienced what could possibly have been your biggest life lesson in patience. You have now resigned yourself to the persistent re-emergence of symptoms. Then, you notice that months have passed with none or very few. At last, your GABA receptors have been repaired and your nervous system is calm again. This is recovery!

I considered myself to be fully recovered when I stopped having waves of symptoms at two years off. I refused to regard it as incomplete recovery because I felt so much better than the tolerance and withdrawal years. Despite my still having the residual hearing distortion and involuntary movements, I was prepared to live a fully functioning life. I knew that my nervous system was in the final stages of its recovery and that these symptoms would eventually disappear. I had the choice of putting my life on hold while I waited, or savouring the return of my vibrance, lucidity and energy. I chose the latter.

The following journal entries chronicle the end of my withdrawal journey:

December 17, 2007

Two-Year Benzo-Free Anniversary

"Today is a significant day for me. In late 2003 I found the *Ashton Manual* online. That marked the beginning of my healing. I then survived a chaotic series of bizarre events spanning a four-year period. They all turned out to be miraculously synchronized and unfolded in perfect order. I am pleased to acknowledge today as being exactly two years since I have been benzo-free.

Yes, two years ago today, I took my last tiny piece of diazepam. Five months earlier, on July 17, 2005, I took my last clonazepam. I have no hesitation in saying that coming off the medication is one of the best decisions I have ever made. Withdrawal, however challenging it may be, is worth enduring when it results in the clarity, coherence and general wellness that I am currently experiencing.

Even with the residual protracted symptoms, I feel one hundred percent better than I did two years ago. And, compared to when I was still on the medication and in tolerance withdrawal, I feel two hundred percent better. I admit that there are times when I have felt a bit impatient because I want all the symptoms to go so I can pronounce myself 'fully recovered'. All I do then is think of how much improved I am. In reality, I am more than fully recovered because I've got 'me' back, the 'me' I almost completely lost during the tolerance years, long before tapering. *Every day in every way I am getting better and better. I am grateful for my healing.*"

January 1, 2008

Clarity

"Today I looked at a photo taken outside my front gate. Although I had always savoured the river's serenity, until recently I had not noticed the ripples in the water. During the bad withdrawal days I would sit outside my door and look at the swans, ducks, birds and weeping willows. It was therapeutic. Now that the depersonalisation, derealisation, brain fog and spaciness have gone, I know that I wasn't able to fully interact or appreciate the beauty through my then blurred eyes and blunt emotions. What I am seeing now is breathtaking; what I am feeling is profound and authentic.

Today, for the first time since tolerance withdrawal, long before I tapered off the clonazepam, I am aware of how much more I am able to truly connect with my surroundings. It feels almost overwhelming to see vivid colours and notice details that were always present but my veiled eyes could not see, at least not through the fog.

I know some of you are still having a difficult time with no windows yet. Sometimes I am hesitant about being too jubilant about my recovery because I do not want to appear insensitive. I do not want you to think I am discounting the fact that it is challenging for you at this time. But I also know that there were times when anyone who was benzo-free and had good news to share would give me more hope in terms of my own healing. This is what I want to achieve by sharing my positive observations. This clarity is worth looking forward to.

In November, when I was dizzy all the time and having an intense set-back, I goaded myself into being patient with no timeline for my recovery. A few months later, I am enjoying this feeling of having 'restored' vision. It is like seeing the world through new eyes."

January 11, 2008
Prosperity

"Often when we read of people's benzo experiences they mention losing everything; I can relate to that. I made a lot of unsound decisions that had devastating repercussions financially but to be benzo-free and resuming a normal life makes it more than worth it.

As withdrawal began to affect me during my second attempt at tapering, I decided to leave the UK and sold both my home and car at a loss. For a long time I couldn't remember what had happened to my hundreds of CDs, DVDs, books and electronic items. Then recently my friends reminded me that I had asked them to take large boxes filled with thousands of pounds worth of items to charity shops or to give them away to anyone who wanted them. They had wondered what was wrong with me at the time. An ex-neighbour told me I had left my front door open and invited them to take all my brand new furniture, appliances and anything else they wanted. I don't remember. During withdrawal I lived off my savings until my accounts were depleted, then family and friends helped to support me.

When I returned close to the end of acute withdrawal, my first few months were spent in bed. I was deep in the throes of withdrawal and felt ill all the time. I could not sit up for more than ten or fifteen minutes at a time. I was staying with a friend, had two bags with a few clothes, three little teddy bears, and my laptop. I had lost everything. I remember thinking, *How did this happen? Where's my stuff? What do I do now? How do I start over?* The withdrawal symptoms were so severe, I knew there was no way I could go out to work. I had to find a way of coping and continued to use positive self-talk, visualisation, affirmations and other techniques to remain optimistic.

Then there was a shift. Something changed and it was liberating. I had nothing external to identify with - no job, no home, no spouse, nothing. I had nowhere to go. I couldn't hop on a plane, I couldn't even go for a walk. But I had 'me' and I was alive. I found a lot of other things to be grateful for. It was empowering, like an awakening, and I began to see my experience as a specially wrapped gift that was priceless. I knew that I would emerge better off physically, mentally, spiritually, emotionally and financially. I didn't need to know how, I just knew.

Today, I am re-acquiring necessities. I seem to need a lot less than I used to, and life is simpler but richer. What matters most is that I have clarity of mind and a nervous system that is beginning to function normally; something no amount of money can buy. Prosperity is about abundance in every area of our lives and I am grateful that I have more than enough of everything I need."

January 16, 2008
Positives About Withdrawal

"It is good to keep remembering that every symptom is evidence that your nervous system is healing. It is readjusting to being fully functional without the drug. You are going through this to get to that place of full recovery. Symptoms are symbolic of the recovery process.

If you have not been able to work, it allows you to get a well-deserved break from the rat-race. You get an opportunity to re-evaluate your work aspirations and even make plans for a career change post-recovery, if that is what you have decided you want.

You may have found that at least one person has turned out to be the most supportive, loyal and non-judgemental friend or family member that anyone could ever ask for. If you have lost connections with others who were unable to support you for whatever reasons, you now have more space in your life to welcome new and harmonious relationships, which you will.

You may have gained confidence as well as renewed respect for your body for having endured withdrawal. You may find that once you are over the shock of the experience, you will have a sense of invincibility and no challenge will ever again phase you.

You may find that the benzo experience has made you tap into your spirituality and has re-ignited your relationship with and belief in a God, Higher Power, Source, Spirit - whatever name you use or concept you have. You now have an unshakable faith and will approach any future obstacles with confidence.

It is possible that you are now *au fait* with coping strategies, techniques, alternative therapies, healthy eating, exercise, and are on your way to being fitter and more balanced in mind, body and spirit than you were before. You have become a walking reference library, well-equipped to help yourself and others.

Things are no longer taken for granted. You may notice feeling pleased and grateful for being able to accomplish a simple task or hobby that at one point, during the worst of withdrawal, you doubted you would ever be able to do again.

If you are experiencing withdrawal, it means you are on your way to creating a new beginning. You can look forward to being benzo-free, to having a clear, lucid mind, a strong, retentive memory, being focused and able to concentrate. Your cognition will no longer be impaired and you will feel like a new person.

Being in withdrawal means you are preparing for a new healthy reality that will give stability, clarity and purpose, and make you open to receiving your good."

The Aftermath

February 10, 2008
From Windows to Open Door

"I am writing this for anyone who is still trying to cope with the brain fog, depersonalisation, derealisation and other psychological and physical symptoms. I am thankful for my current window of clarity which I think has become my open door to recovery. It has now been ten weeks. The continuous lucidity and clarity of thought are still slightly unfamiliar. It feels pleasantly strange after having spent the last ten years in a blurred reality. My recovery still makes me feel emotional and extremely pleased. I feel as if I have been given a second chance at life.

Not very long ago, I was having one of my worst withdrawal waves. Despite affirming and remaining positive, there was a tiny part of me that wondered whether I should just accept that I may either have permanent brain damage or, that I may have a few more years to wait for my recovery. A little voice tried to reason that maybe it was part of my reality, a path I needed to take, and if I affirmed otherwise, it was my ego getting in the way. I resisted those fears

and continued affirming my healing and speaking positive-
ly to myself. A bigger voice inside responded saying, "Be
patient; you will make your own happy ending."

I started challenging myself to do a lot of the activities I
had postponed for when I got better – anything that I was
capable of doing. I stopped giving attention to the symp-
toms, acting, even if in mind only, as if I had no symptoms.
This was difficult with the dizziness and hearing problems
but there was a part of me that just would not give in to
that other voice telling me withdrawal has gone on for
much too long and it must be something more.

If any of this resonates with you, I cannot tell you with
any more conviction that your healing is taking place, now,
as you read this. When a symptom seems unrelenting and
you have done everything possible and nothing seems to be
working, trust that your brain is in the process of readjust-
ing to being functional without the drug. Then imagine
what you will be like (go into as much detail as possible and
feel it as well) without the foggy brain or whatever your
symptoms are. See yourself doing all the things you cannot
yet do but will be able to when the symptoms go.

When I read what I had written in November and think
of how I feel now, I cannot help but write to remind you
that every day in every way your body is recovering. Your
healing has already taken place."

March 20, 2008
"Yes" to Wellness

"Withdrawal? What withdrawal? I haven't had any
waves of symptoms and am beginning to forget my experi-
ence. Yes! Benzo withdrawal is temporary. If you are still
having a challenging time, trust that your recovery is taking

place even as you read this. It really is! After many years of tolerance withdrawal and two years of acute then protracted withdrawal, this phoenix has risen.

Lately, I have had these feelings of invincibility as if I can do anything. I am being sensible though. Instead of attempting a marathon or anything too extreme, I have been gradually introducing simple changes. The numbness and tingling which lasted for years disappeared spontaneously and now, apart from the distorted hearing and involuntary movements, I am well.

That brings me to the often asked question: "What is full recovery?" I am ninety five percent symptom free and consider myself to be fully recovered. Yes, I still have these few symptoms, but compared to the numerous ones that I had throughout, they are insignificant. Plus I feel better than I did for the entire time I was on the drug. Once I have no recurring waves and am free of anger, resentment, blame or guilt, I can say "yes" to my wellness. My benzo journey is over. Life goes on - residual symptoms or not - and every day has the potential to be joy-filled. That is how it will be for me.

No matter what symptoms you are having, no matter how frustrated, scared or out of control you might be feeling, what is happening to the mind and body, for most of us, is temporary. These symptoms disappear, the nervous system recovers and life resumes normality."

April 19, 2008
Relationships

"When I think of my relationships – those that survived, those I have lost and new ones I have made, I have no regrets. I think about my caring, loyal family members and friends who supported me throughout the tolerance and withdrawal years, and am overcome with deep gratitude. I feel so honoured to have had their attention and care. I do not know how I would have coped otherwise.

I also think about others who found my experience too much to cope with and avoided contact. In some cases I did too, as I did not have the emotional energy to expend at the time. Coping simultaneously with withdrawal and the more demanding relationships can be emotionally draining. It was necessary for me to let them go. Stress-reduction was my objective and it worked. I have released these relationships with love.

If some friends or family members become unavailable and inaccessible during your withdrawal, it could be because they are unable to relate to your experience or they simply cannot cope. You may be able to reconcile some of these relationships after you recover or you may have to lovingly release them from your life. What you will find is a special gift - that of being surrounded by people who genuinely and unconditionally care. You will also find that you are now left with ample space in your life to accommodate new, loving relationships.

I am grateful for the relationships that have been strengthened as a result of my experience, for the new friendships I have made, and for being unconditionally loved and supported. I am grateful too, for my recovery and being able to reciprocate."

May 8, 2008

Racking My Brain

"I keep saying that one day benzo withdrawal will be a distant memory but how do I know this to be true? It is because my lucidity, coherence, cognitive faculties and physical stamina have been so fully restored that hard as I try, I can barely recall what having brain fog and all the other symptoms was like.

Today I will reiterate the fact that no matter where you are in your recovery process, the day will come when you will once again feel well. You will be so busy resuming your normal activities, you won't give withdrawal a thought, or you will have to struggle to remember what it was like.

I vaguely remember what my days of tolerance, acute and protracted withdrawal were like. I read through my journals and old logs and have very little recollection with no negative emotions. I know that for a brief period late in my recovery stage I recognised some strong post-traumatic type emotions. I felt shell-shocked and kept thinking, *How on earth did this happen to me?* But along with my physical healing my spirit has healed and is lighter than before, and now I celebrate the content, grounded, post-benzo me. You will too.

You may be experiencing brain fog, adrenaline surges, feelings of depersonalisation and derealisation, distorted visual or tactile perception and other psychological and physical benzo withdrawal symptoms. In a few months or possibly (but hopefully not) years, you will look back at this time and think, *I can't remember what withdrawal was like.*

I have been writing online for more than a year. I smile when I think that some of my benzo friends who were distraught about their unrelenting symptoms and emailed me for many months are fully recovered. They are preoccupied with their families, back at work, or so busy in general that

I either don't hear from them or I get a keep in touch email once in a while.

I am always pleased when a regular visitor stops logging on to this site because it is no longer necessary. Quite a few of our benzo friends whose relationships ended because of the benzo issue have met new people. One gentleman emailed me today to say he has met someone new and is engaged to be married.

I know it can be challenging at times to see past your withdrawal experience. Please remember that benzo withdrawal is a syndrome and not a medical condition for which you will need continuous treatment. It is temporary in most cases. It will strengthen your character and resolve, your nervous system will recover and be restored to full functionality. You will, one day, have to rack your brains to remember what your experience was like. If you are feeling discouraged, please keep these thoughts in mind."

May 19, 2008

All Is Well

"I am pleased to share that I am still enjoying my recovery with no recurrence of withdrawal symptoms. I keep improving daily and feel better than I have in many years. Withdrawal waves and windows are no more. It has been an open door into the world of coherence and lucidity for which I am grateful. I know that when the timing is right, you too, will be celebrating your recovery.

I still have the intermittent drug-induced dyskinesia and my hearing remains distorted but I have no complaints. It is pure bliss to have my cognitive faculties back, to be able to complete a sentence, to think clearly and to remember what I am looking for or where I put it.

So, here I am again, the broken record, reminding you that if you are still experiencing withdrawal symptoms, they will go as soon as your receptors re-establish their affinity for GABA and your nervous system has recovered. Like me, you will keep improving until you are fully healed."

June 15, 2008
How I Knew it was Over

"While I can't recall an exact date, here is the sequence of events that led me to the realisation that withdrawal was finally over. I had my first window of clarity early on in withdrawal – approximately three months after the end of my complete taper. It lasted a short time and throughout the next two years a pattern of windows and waves developed.

Close to the end of the second year, along with the spasms and hearing problems, I started having some surprisingly severe waves with extreme dizziness and other symptoms. I knew though, that withdrawal was coming to an end especially because my clarity, coherence and cognitive faculties were significantly improving.

I had to learn to not anticipate a window or wave. I relinquished control and just observed the process, trusting that the outcome would be good. I did not resist and kept reminding myself that in spite of all the madness, all the inconsistencies and surprises, I was recovering. I regarded the disturbances as evidence that my nervous system's fine-tuning was taking place.

Then, around the two-year mark I had influenza and it did not trigger a withdrawal wave as would have been the case during the first eighteen months of withdrawal. For the next few months the window continued and I was more lucid and coherent than I had been throughout the tolerance and withdrawal years. It was a gradual observation. I felt that if more than three months passed without a wave of symptoms, then surely it must mean recovery. That was indeed the case.

I hope that this will happen for you too. Even if it seems to be taking forever, the brain fog and other symptoms do not usually last indefinitely. The thing about withdrawal is that there is no logic, set pattern, reason or rhyme to it. This is why patience, non-anticipation, non-resistance and hope are our best companions throughout this journey. The only thing we know for certain is that withdrawal is temporary and in time, most of us recover."

June 17, 2008
The Calm After the Storm

"There is another dimension to the aftermath of withdrawal. Earlier this year during the first few months of no waves, apart from being elated and relieved, I felt slightly shell-shocked and shaken. Withdrawal for me was like having a category five hurricane arrive without warning and having to run inside for shelter, but instead of it lasting hours it lasted two and a half years.

The windows of clarity were akin to the calm that one experiences when the eye of the storm is passing. The waves of symptoms were the high, destructive winds. All I could do was accept my fate, curl up on the sofa and wait for the fury to subside.

At last the storm passed, and I emerged from the rubble feeling grateful for having survived. I looked at the debris and the material damage but felt no sense of loss because I was alive and well. I was feeling better than I had during the tolerance years when the storm was brewing. I consider that period just after the last wave to be my post-trauma period.

Now, almost six months later, I am still in awe of the clarity, lucidity and physical wellness that I am experiencing. I cannot articulate the sense of peace that my experience has brought me. The many days of not being able to go out or even to read left me with no option but to breathe and be still.

I know that coping with benzo withdrawal is a big challenge. Yet, so far, many of us who have now moved on confirm that withdrawal has set us up for life in terms of the lessons and revelations. Learning patience, compassion and appreciation for the simplest things in life are invaluable gifts.

Most of us do not regret having had this experience because once you have recovered you are inclined to think: *Wow, I survived. I made it. I am amazing. I can handle anything now.* It makes the everyday challenges of life seem insignificant. As one friend who is now recovered said, "Life after benzos is a piece of cake."

You may be feeling shell-shocked because this experience is so surreal, was not anticipated, and literally threw your equilibrium off. It will help if you are able to relax into the present moment, symptoms and all, and remember that you are being set up for life. When this is over, nothing will phase you."

June 22, 2008
Winds of Change

"Today is an unusually windy day in South Wales with extremely high gusts. Outside my home are two big weeping willow trees which line the water's edge. I've grown quite attached to them especially to the larger of the two, the branches of which hang near my windows.

As I gaze outside I can see the less flexible trees and other plants losing leaves and branches as they resist the wind, but my dear weeping willows are simply swaying, dancing, moving to and fro, making beautiful music in the process.

As I enjoy the windsong, my mind wanders to the withdrawal experience and I feel moved to write about it. When we go against the wind, we become tense, rigid and more susceptible to the pressure. When we gently ease into the flow and not resist, we are less likely to 'break' and tend to have a smoother emotional path to recovery.

May the winds of your challenge soon take you back to that place of wellness. As your journey progresses, may you be filled with acceptance and courage. May you also have hope, peace and even find opportunities to make good music and dance along the way."

July 3, 2008
Wellness is our Natural State of Being

"It is now the seventh month of my recovery from benzodiazepine withdrawal. I had no inkling that this adventure of a lifetime would have resulted from my flippantly waltzing into my doctors office, that morning in 1998, concerned that a simple tic of my eyelid would ruin my wedding.

I am still amazed at my body's resilience and its natural ability to heal. Yes, I am still having the involuntary spasms and hearing issues but oh how well I feel, and how much more content I am. Had I not been logging my experience, I would not have remembered much. If you are finding coping with your symptoms challenging, please take heart in what I am writing today.

After having had the brain fog and other cognitive issues during the tolerance years and then the intensification during acute and post-withdrawal, I seriously experienced moments of underlying doubt, and sometimes wondered whether I was in denial and should I not accept that this is how I will be permanently experiencing my new world. (This tends to happen to those whose symptoms persist longer than expected.)

Having worked in the mental health field, I knew that the brain fog and some of the other psychological symptoms form the blurred reality through which many people navigate their daily lives. I thought maybe it was my fate too. I was not depressed or even upset when I had these thoughts, I just wanted to be 'realistic' and non-resistant. I felt inclined to plan how I was going to make the best of a life observed through what seemed like a veil or smoke screen.

Then, January came and the clarity kept improving daily. As the months went by I began to experience my pre-benzo coherence and lucidity. I still find it fascinating that one little pill could make such an impact on every aspect of a person's life. I can never run out of things to be grateful for because every day I have constant reminders of how well-recovered I am.

Yesterday, for the first time since withdrawal, I noticed the ringing in my ears (tinnitus) had stopped. I was agog and at a loss for words. It didn't last long, only about ten minutes, but I was thrilled. Experiencing that intense silence was remarkable. I know that there is a bit more 're-pair work' to be done and so I trust that this will be resolved in time.

If you have been waiting for months or even years for the fog to lift and for your psychological and physical symptoms to go, please trust that your recovery is on schedule.

Try to be patient and not resist the changes that are taking place. Practise positive self-talk and other coping tools, nurture yourself well, and then sit back and allow the major overhaul (GABA/receptor issue) and then fine-tuning to take place. Know that one day, like me, you will be reflecting on the times when you thought you would not have survived, and you will smile and shake your head and think, *Yes, I did it!*"

❧17❧

Closure

The nightmare has ended. The waves of symptoms gradually became shorter and the windows of clarity longer. Or, maybe you had very few or no windows and woke up one morning to find all the symptoms gone. Still, you are hesitant to claim your recovery. What if, as in the past, you declare full recovery only to be swept away by another wave? Then you think, *No, it has been months since I've had a flare-up; this must be it.* Yes, this *is* it! The moment you have dreamt of for what seemed like forever has finally arrived.

Your precious receptors have been repaired and have regained their affinity for the calming GABA; your nervous system is no longer in overdrive and is functioning well without the drug. Even if one or two symptoms are still persisting, once the waves of intense symptoms have gone and you are feeling well for a prolonged period, there is no harm in claiming your recovery. You can now pronounce yourself recovered. Whether full or incomplete, you can exhale. You are now, once again, in control of your life.

You coped successfully through benzo withdrawal and that means not only are you a survivor, you have proven how strong, courageous and amazing a person you are. This is no time for modesty; benzo withdrawal was a monumental challenge and you've made it through to the very end. Congratulations!

The absence of symptoms, however, is only one aspect of recovery. There may be a few more hurdles to overcome on the way to achieving a genuine state of complete healing. A problematic withdrawal can be so devastating, it is no surprise that letting go of the experience can sometimes be difficult for some.

People react differently to the realisation of recovery. After receiving confirmation that withdrawal is over, some are left feeling shell-shocked and traumatised for a while. In an effort to forget the experience others refuse to talk about it or relive it in any way. For them, this is closure. Others spend a long time after recovery trying to come to terms with their losses. They may have lost prime years of their lives, relationships and property; this makes starting over challenging.

Recognising and processing these losses may be a necessary path to healing. Problems arise when one over-identifies and remains attached to the experience and the associated negative emotions become ingrained in the psyche. This results in an inability to move on. The preoccupation with the benzo experience ends up lasting indefinitely, and although the symptoms have permanently subsided, the person continues to feel generally unwell. Counselling can be beneficial for anyone faced with this obstacle.

You may be concerned about an antidepressant or other drug that you may be taking and are yet to taper off. Don't worry, the worst is over. Benzo withdrawal is the most intense of all.

If you plan on promoting awareness about benzodiazepines, it is best to consider doing this after your emotional healing has taken place. The negatives associated with the experience should be released in order for physical and emotional wellness to be maintained. Although benzo withdrawal may have already stolen a few or many years of your life, it is now time to let it go in order to create room for the good that awaits you.

Stigmatisation

One aspect of the aftermath of withdrawal which may be surprising is how quickly one can be judged and stigmatised. I remember feeling misunderstood when an old friend immediately recoiled once I shared my experience. She lectured me about being 'on guard' and not 'giving in' to my cravings, then avoided me. This is a typical reaction.

Stigmatisation involves labelling someone because of a condition or an experience, stereotyping and devaluing the person. Some benzo ex-users may find that despite having been prescribed the drug, acquiring it legally and not having had cravings, they are still subject to the stigma that goes with being considered a drug 'addict'. This stigmatisation is based on ignorance and lack of awareness and will be perpetuated until benzo issues are acknowledged and addressed.

Although the symptoms that you have experienced were withdrawal-induced, many may not regard this as a legitimate medical conclusion. You may therefore be judged as creating your withdrawal problems through your own choices and actions. Don't be disappointed if no one is interested in finding out whether or not you were given the option of making an informed decision when the drug was initially prescribed. There is nothing to be ashamed of. You were prescribed a drug and were unaware of its effects. Benzo dependency and iatrogenic addiction can affect anyone and any family; no one is exempt.

Again, due to lack of awareness, the magnitude of the issues you have overcome may go unacknowledged and you may not receive the deserved recognition. Don't be perturbed; those of us who have survived withdrawal know that we are remarkably resilient, strong and courageous.

We also know stigmatisation exists. So, how then do we cope? First, you are not obligated to share your experience. You can decide how much to disclose and to whom. You may be comfortable speaking to certain family members and friends, or you may decide to talk about it only if absolutely necessary. The most important thing is to not let fear or anticipation of being stigmatised lead to social isolation. Even if you choose not to discuss your experience, it is important to stay in touch with those who care about you. You do not want to end up losing much needed attention and support.

You may, like me, feel extremely proud of overcoming your dependency and surviving withdrawal. This could lead to your decision to actively challenge stigma and to promote benzo awareness within your wider circle of family and friends. Or, you may opt for tackling the bigger issues by joining the existing 'army' of awareness lobbyists, setting up a website or giving support within the benzo community.

Energy channelled into promoting benzodiazepine awareness, lobbying and supporting others can be beneficial, is badly needed and always welcome.

Return of Underlying Condition

One question which is frequently asked during withdrawal or after recovery is whether or not the underlying condition for which the drug was prescribed will return. It may have been prescribed for an anxiety-related condition because of a transitory response to a traumatic life event such as a bereavement and the user ended up taking it for a much longer period than intended. The best scenario is that the ex-user is pleasantly surprised to find that the underlying condition is gone; this happens quite often. If there is a return of the underlying condition, depending on what it is, there are other options.

Those who were prescribed benzos for chronic anxiety or other psychological issues may now resolve that no matter what lies ahead, they will be able to follow a non-pharmacological route leading to other ways of coping. They may not have been aware of many of these methods prior to taking the drug. What could have once been regarded as too simple solutions: breathing practices, guided imagery, emotional freedom techniques (EFT), meditation, progressive relaxation and other self-management tools learned during withdrawal, have become invaluable alternatives. Some become experts at grounding themselves and using positive self-talk to remain calm. Others who may not be able to successfully apply these types of self-help techniques find cognitive behavioural therapy (CBT) and other forms of counselling to be useful.

Many ex-users feel a strong sense of accomplishment after having survived withdrawal. The issue for which they were prescribed the benzo now seems insignificant in comparison to the multitude of problems faced and conquered during withdrawal. Being able to have successfully dealt with the bizarre physical and psychological symptoms gives them new confidence.

Letting Go and Accepting 'Now'

Depending on the duration of your benzo use and recovery period, you may be starting over after a very long break from 'normal' life. My benzo adventure began in 1998 and I confirmed my recovery in early 2008. When I was first prescribed the drug my waist measured twenty-five inches, I had fewer wrinkles and higher energy levels. Because I was in a fog for most of the ten years of my experience, I went through a phase post-recovery where I wanted to back-track and pick up from Spring 1998. It was not possible and I quickly had to accept that withdrawal or not, I would have had other challenges and I also would have aged! Being realistic is liberating.

If you are a few pounds heavier with little aches and pains, please don't let this prevent you from enjoying your recovery. You may have gaps in your memory, your skin and hair may be different and there may also be a few other unwelcome changes. Despite all of this, you are alive and well and most of all, benzo-free.

Even if one or two minor symptoms are persisting, you can make the most of the good health that you now enjoy and continue to effect new changes. After I realised the waves of symptoms were no longer re-emerging, I mentioned to a friend that I was feeling much better but still had distorted hearing and involuntary movements. He shared that he had had tinnitus and hearing hypersensitivity for the past fifteen years. I was surprised as he had never mentioned it. He lives a full and exciting life, and does not allow the hearing distortion to impede him. It helped me to put my recovery into perspective. I knew then, that I did not need to wait for those residual symptoms to abate in order for me to celebrate the end of withdrawal. Having improved cognition and no waves of symptoms was enough for me to claim my recovery and start afresh.

Regaining Confidence

Not everyone emerges from the withdrawal experience with elevated self-worth. Some feel remorseful and blame themselves for not having been more vigilant. They regret not having researched the drug or asking the initial prescribing doctor more questions. Others think, *How could I have let this happen?* Please do not let guilt affect your emotional healing.

Still, if there is a need to rationalise, you can consider this: Now that you have been through withdrawal, you, more than anyone, are aware of the general lack of awareness regarding benzodiazepines. How then could you, an average layperson, have known about the dependency properties of the drug? It is most likely that you were experiencing a traumatic event or some other serious life situation and needed help; you were not looking for an illegal drug to have a 'fix'. You made what seemed to have been the best decision based on the choices and information you were given at the time. You did not 'let it happen'. Please let go of any self-blame you may be feeling. 'It' happened and you beat it! That is all that matters now. This experience is now a proud part of your past.

Now is the time to acknowledge your exceptional accomplishment. What you have just experienced, if seen from a positive perspective, can turn out to be your biggest confidence booster. You made the decision to quit a highly addictive substance. You found the courage and determination to taper. If you cold-turkeyed, not only were you brave, you had 'someone' watching over you. You then coped with acute and post-acute withdrawal.

Try not to look outside of yourself for commendation. It is difficult for anyone who has not been through benzo withdrawal (not cocaine, heroin, alcohol or any other) to appreciate the magnitude of the challenge and the complex dynamics involved. If you have fully or incompletely recovered from benzo withdrawal, you deserve to have the highest self-esteem possible.

Wherever your experience takes you, always remember that you have overcome an immense challenge. You have successfully coped with benzo withdrawal and are now once again in control of your life. You do not need to justify what transpired, convince anyone that withdrawal was not 'all in your head', feel embarrassed or humiliated. You can release any negative aspects of this experience knowing that you are a survivor, a winner and an extremely remarkable person. All that is left for you to do now is exhale, let go of the drama and enjoy your new beginning. Life awaits your presence.

∞18∞

Success Stories

Writing a benzo success story involves reliving an unpleasant experience which may trigger unwanted memories. It is fully understandable then, that after dealing with withdrawal many people don't ever want to hear the word 'benzo' again. They simply want to make up for lost time, resume their normal lives and forget about withdrawal. This is why recovered ex-users should never be pressured to share their stories, and why I am so grateful to those who have done so here.

Mike

Mike took diazepam (Valium) for two years. His wife, Mary, took it for almost nine. When Mary noticed that her memory and reading comprehension were being affected, they both decided to quit. Although Mary was on it for much longer, they tapered using similar schedules over the same period of time. They both took supplements during their tapers but ended up having very different recovery processes.

Mary had very few symptoms and, after four months of what she describes as mild discomfort, felt better than all her years on the drug. She was benzo-free and fully recovered. Mike, on the other hand, had the most distressing symptoms. He had pains all over his body, with the head and back pain being almost unbearable. He also experienced many of the psychological symptoms and found the depersonalisation, derealisation, brain fog and obsessive thoughts in particular, very disturbing. Sadly, these symptoms remained with him for more than three years. He could not understand how his wife had healed so quickly and why his symptoms were so unrelenting.

It was not until his thirty-second month off that Mike experienced his first 'window'. His wife could not accept that the drug could have had such an effect. She eventually concluded that something else must be wrong with him. All diagnostic tests were negative and Mike resolved to accept his symptoms and allow his healing to take place. He feels that his faith, regular use of breathing exercises and positive self-talk helped him to cope.

When Mike experienced his first few months of being symptom free he was so worried about a flare-up, he did not tell anyone. He was thrilled but tentative - always in fear of something going wrong. He'd spent such a long time feeling unwell, his recovery was at first very surreal. He admits that for a while, he did not know how to move on. It has now been seven months since Mike's recovery and, thankfully, he has not had the return of even one symptom. Life is back to normal for him, and he and Mary are planning a cruise this summer.

William

William was prescribed lorazepam (Ativan) over a period of three and a half months to deal with anxiety which resulted from a traumatic event. He was also taking the antidepressant, venlaflexine (Effexor). Although he felt he was on lorazepam for a short time, he very sensibly opted to taper off by making very, very small cuts over a six-month period. During his taper he started experiencing stomach pains, restless legs, intense feelings of exhaustion, cog fog, muscle and joint pains, severe depression, insomnia, severe headaches and skin pain which made him feel permanently sunburnt.

He eventually made it to being benzo-free and at three months off, started having mood swings with feelings of rage. His antidepressant was no longer effective and although he continued taking it, his depression worsened. There was no light at the end of the tunnel for William. He was scared. The nightmare stories that he found on the internet combined with having this problematic withdrawal made him feel like giving up. He even considered reinstating the lorazepam, but decided not to.

One morning, he woke up feeling as if he was healing. This was his first window. He went on to have what he called "good days and bad days." Eventually he was improved enough to return to work. At seven months off lorazepam, William felt fully recovered and was able to focus on tapering off the antidepressant. He felt that having survived benzo withdrawal, he was more than equipped to deal with quitting the venlaflexine.

A year later, William was off all medication. He says that he no longer takes his health for granted and eats healthily, exercises regularly and practises meditation and yoga for relaxation. He has just completed counselling to work on the issue for which he was first prescribed the medication, and now feels optimistic and in control of his life again.

Annie

Annie had terrible burning sensations, obsessive thoughts and insomnia which all surfaced during her taper off clonazepam (Klonopin/Rivotril) which she took for eleven years. She did not have any early 'windows' of clarity and the symptoms had been relentless.

"I gave up on ever being able to sleep properly again. Never had more than two hours since coming off Klonopin three and a half years ago. I was always agitated. I had two awful thoughts that stayed with me the whole time. I felt I would have them forever. The burning was so intense all I could do sometimes was lie in the tub in cool water. It would make it bearable for a while. I cried every day. Monday, I noticed the thoughts were gone. Now the burning is gone and last night I slept for more than seven hours.

I am crying now but this time it is not because I am scared or sad. I feel like this is a rebirth. It is taking time to sink in. This is a miracle. I refused psychiatric treatment because I knew it had to be withdrawal. I was taking Klonopin for anxiety and they told me the anxiety came back and this is why I was having the thoughts. When my doctor said maybe I have OCD I was scared. Now my mind is quiet for the first time in years. I am in shock. This is awesome."

The burning, insomnia and thoughts never returned. Annie now uses several approaches including Emotional Freedom Techniques (EFT) and breathing to cope with her anxiety. She has just completed a college diploma and has started a new job.

Charlotta

Charlotta was prescribed 0.5 mg alprazolam (Xanax) three times daily for anxiety related to a family bereavement. She quickly developed a tolerance and the dosage was increased. This kept happening over a period of six years until she was taking 8 mg daily. Her withdrawal problems began during these periods of tolerance and she thought she had developed a serious psychological problem.

When her doctor stopped increasing the dose and tolerance withdrawal once again set in, she got her husband to have her admitted to a mental health institution. They stopped her medication without tapering. What Charlotte experienced during the cold-turkey detox was too disturbing to be shared here; it was extremely traumatic for her. She was faced with every conceivable symptom and more. It was only after her discharge when her husband found the *Ashton Manual* online, that they realised the benzo was the source of her all problems.

At two years and six months off she was experiencing nausea, blurred vision, severe head pressure, head pain, confusion, dizziness, fatigue, restless legs at night, tinnitus, constant muscle spasms in her leg, constipation, benzo belly, burning pains in her leg that would come and go, stiff and painful neck with a burning spine, memory problems, repetitive thoughts, difficulty understanding conversations, itchy rash and withdrawal-induced depression.

Most of these symptoms came in waves but some were constant. Around thirty-four months off she noticed that some were beginning to lessen in intensity. However, it wasn't long before she was hit with a very intense wave of severe symptoms. She described it as worse than any of the previous waves had been. Although she was thrown and very discouraged by this setback, she kept telling herself that her healing was taking place. This was difficult with the withdrawal-induced depression but she could not allow herself to give up hope. She had already been through so much, her situation could only improve.

Soon after the three-year mark, the restless legs, repetitive thoughts and muscle spasms suddenly stopped. She was, at last, able to sleep for more than two hours each night. Other symptoms persisted but she was beginning to feel much improved. At thirty-eight months off, more symptoms disappeared and she was left with just blurred vision, dizziness and the itchy rash.

A few months later, at approximately forty-one months off, Charlotta felt that despite the odd symptom surfacing for very short periods, she was completely healed. She was ecstatic. After such a long period of terrible insomnia, she was enjoying many hours of sound, refreshing sleep. The silence after the tinnitus was, according to her, "like heaven." Being symptom free and back in charge of her life was a joy for her. She even joked about her husband not being able to stop celebrating the return of his beloved wife. The best thing for Charlotta was knowing that she did not have permanent damage which was her greatest fear during the whole journey. For her, life after benzos is the "coolest" ever because "nothing sucks" and "everything is great!"

Seren

Seren was nineteen when she was first prescribed lorazepam (Ativan) for panic attacks. She quickly developed tolerance and the dosage was periodically increased until she was on 10 mg daily. After eleven years on the drug, Seren began to feel much worse than when she initially took it. She experienced cognitive and other problems and, as she said, "was in a total mess." Her doctor was reluctant to help her discontinue the drug and she decided to taper off without his assistance. She tapered off over a two-month period. She was worried about missing work, was not aware of the Ashton or any other method, and just wanted to be benzo free.

Seren had a very intense withdrawal with just about every conceivable symptom. She refers to this as "true benzo hell." During her third year off she became very frustrated and quite depressed at what she felt was slow progress. She was still experiencing terrible brain fog, muscle pain with burning, insomnia, high anxiety, mood swings and a host of other problems. She felt that her worst symptom was the terrible feeling of impending doom. Most of her family and friends were no longer interested in her "drama" which they felt was self-inflicted. Seren said that on many occasions she felt like giving up and was worried that she would sink into a deep depression or give in to the suicidal repetitive thoughts she was having at the time.

Thankfully, in early 2008 she stumbled upon the old *Lights In My Windows* website and for the first time in years, began to feel encouraged. She started doing the diaphragmatic breathing technique and kept talking to herself positively. She wasn't keen on affirmations but found that positively talking herself through the symptoms had stirred something deep inside her. A will to survive her nightmare was ignited.

A few months later, Seren experienced her first 'window' of clarity. She was overjoyed but also quite tentative and still unsure of her recovery. It was a brief window and another wave soon came crashing. This setback threw her off-course; she said it almost broke her completely. It was also at that time that Seren became more determined than ever to survive. She felt that letting go of the process was important and made the decision to totally surrender. That way, she would be allowing her recovery to unfold in its own time. She started to observe her symptoms without becoming upset. Though they persisted for a few more months, this new attitude made the experience a lot less unpleasant that it had previously been.

By late 2008 Seren's symptoms started disappearing. She hesitated to mention her progress in case they returned. After being four months symptom-free she was convinced of her recovery. Seren is now in her mid-thirties. She lost a lot of her prime years to lorazepam but is relieved that that chapter of her life is over. She is happy to be given another change and is carving a new life for herself. What has been her biggest blessing is that since her recovery, she has had no panic episodes or any return of the pre-existing anxiety. She has been using all the coping techniques she learned during withdrawal to cope with her 'underlying' condition and has no intentions of ever again taking medication for anxiety.

Carrie

Carrie is a single parent with three children. She took a combination of diazepam (Valium) and the z-drug, eszopiclone (Lunesta) for four and a half years. Her doctor initially prescribed zopiclone for insomnia but she very quickly developed tolerance. She then started buying Valium via the internet as she felt it would help her to cope with the effects of the Lunesta. Carrie said she gradually became a "zombie" and found it challenging to look after her children.

When Carrie cold-turkeyed first off eszopiclone and later, diazepam, she became very ill and suffered severe withdrawal symptoms. Despite this, she had to find a way to appear as normal as possible for the sake of her children. She had no family and very few friends who could support her and as her condition worsened, the threat of having her children taken into care hovered. The eldest of the three children, her eleven year-old daughter, temporarily assumed the role of main caregiver and looked after her younger siblings. Although Carrie tried to explain that "Mommy was feeling a bit sick but would be better soon," the youngest kept asking, "Are you going to die?" For Carrie, this was heartbreaking. She knew her withdrawal was making her children feel that no one was available to take care of them - something which was not far from the truth.

As withdrawal persisted, Carrie's ability to cope lessened. She could not focus well enough to assist the children with homework, attend activities, cook or do anything required of a parent. Without the help of her friend who eventually took the children to stay with her family, Carrie feels that she would have been left with no option but to have the children's services intervene.

After being benzo-free and in withdrawal for twenty-eight months, Carrie experienced her first days of feeling slightly improved. She was eager to have her children return home but had to wait another five months before they were able to do so. It took another six months before she felt any optimism about recovering.

It has now been four years since Carrie has been off both drugs. She has now returned to full-time work and actively participates in her children's lives. She still has a few minor issues but considers herself to be fully recovered. Her home and family life are once again secure and stable.

James

After taking clonazepam (Klonopin/Rivotril) for fourteen months, James began to feel unwell. He was on a low dose of .125 mg daily and did a quick taper off, with no supervision. He had a relatively intense acute period with distorted perception, intense pain and burning, nausea and dizziness. At six months off he developed gastric problems, persistent low back pains, recurring obsessive thoughts, stitch-like cramp below his ribs, loss of appetite, high anxiety, paranoid and depressive moods.

His back pain was very severe and as a result he had diagnostic tests to rule out a suspected kidney stone. He also had other diagnostic tests which were all negative. When he consulted a psychiatrist, he was told that his symptoms could not possibly be related to withdrawal because his dose was low. James became frustrated and was convinced he was mentally ill. Based on his doctors' opinions, there was no way his problems could have been caused by the clonazepam.

After exchanging a few emails via the website, James felt reassured that what he was experiencing was indeed due to his withdrawal. He was encouraged to try breathing and other relaxation techniques and also experimented with positive self-talk. Despite this, he felt that he was barely hanging on to his sanity and at times became convinced that he must be very, very ill with some unknown disease.

James had very few 'windows' during his first year of being benzo-free. He felt discouraged because many of his online friends who had been on higher doses for longer, were already having periods of feeling improved. He tried a few supplements and was disappointed and discouraged when he had a most intense flare-up of symptoms. This 'wave' continued until his sixteenth month off, when he had finally had a good window. More setbacks followed, but by his twenty-seventh month off, he began to feel better than he had for many years. He knew then, that his full recovery was imminent. It was, and James' life is back to normal. He is now engaged to be married to an old friend who proved to be "his rock" during his benzo ordeal.

Happy endings are always encouraging. The most difficult stories to obtain are from ex-users who had no problems or just very few, mild symptoms. As previously mentioned, most of them do not frequent the internet forums or benzo websites and some are not aware that benzo withdrawal exists. However, all you really need to know is that there are numerous success stories and most people do recover from benzo withdrawal. Like the many thousands before you, including me and these survivors who have shared here, you will overcome your benzo issues, your nervous system will heal, and you will, one day, celebrate your recovery.

In recognition of the work
of Professor C. Heather Ashton

Professor C. Heather Ashton is an unsung heroine and the person who, through her careful and responsible advice given in the *Ashton Manual*, helped me to identify what was making me ill. I do not know how many lives she has saved or prevented from further harm through her work with benzodiazepines but I would easily imagine tens of thousands.

Professor Ashton DM, FRCP is Emeritus Professor of Clinical Psycho-pharmacology at the University of Newcastle upon Tyne, England. For decades she has researched the effects of psychotropic drugs including benzodiazepines and from 1982 to 1994 her main clinical work was in running a benzodiazepine withdrawal clinic. Her manual is to-date the most comprehensive guide for withdrawing from benzodiazepines.

Our website has received hundreds of emails which include the lines, "...it was only when I read the *Ashton Manual* that I began to under-stand..." We honestly do not know how the many people in 'Benzo-land' would have fared, had they not used the *Ashton Manual* to successfully taper and to convince their well-intentioned doctors that their symptoms were not 'all in the head'.

On behalf of all of us who have benefited from your work, we whole-heartedly thank you, Professor Ashton.

Appendix 1
Resources Guide

Benzodiazepine Books and CDs

Updated 2007 version of the *Ashton Manual* by Prof. C H Ashton can be purchased at www.benzobookreview.com/ashton.html or the 2002 version can be downloaded from Ray Nimmo's website at www.benzo.org.uk/manual.

The Benzo Book by Jack Hobson-Dupont is available on Amazon or at www.thebenzobook.com.

Safe Benzo Withdrawal CD by Paula Kovacs comprises an easy listening audio complete with a relaxation exercise, and a data-read only CD which includes printable PDFs of Professor Ashton's withdrawal schedules. Both have been specifically written for benzo withdrawal. Website: www.benzorecovery.co.uk

The www.benzo.org.uk website lists all current books on benzodiazepines and how they can be purchased. Some of these can be bought online at the www.benzobookreview.com website.

Benzodiazepine Forums (Fora)

Benzo Buddies: www.benzobuddies.org

Benzo Island: http://benzoisland.org/index.html

Benzo Liberty: www.benzoliberty.com

Benzo Withdrawal.Com: http://benzowithdrawal.com/forum

Yahoo Benzo Withdrawal Support Group: http://health.groups.yahoo.com/group/benzo

Tranquilliser Recovery and Awareness Place (TRAP): www.thetrap.org.uk/forum

Benzodiazepine Helplines

Battle Against Tranquillisers
National Helpline Tel: 0117 966 3629
Website: www.bataid.org

Bristol and District Tranquilliser Project
National Helpline Tel: 0117 962 8874

Council Against Involuntary Tranquilliser Addiction (CITA)
National Helpline Tel: 0151 932 0102
Website: www.citawithdrawal.org.uk

MIND in Camden Minor Tranquilliser Service
(serves boroughs of Camden and Islington, London)
Helpline: 0207 911 0816
Website: http://www.mindincamden.org.uk/mtproject.htm

Benzodiazepine Websites

Benzo.org/Ray Nimmo's website: www.benzo.org.uk

Benzo Withdrawal Support: www.benzosupport.org

Benzodiazepines Co-operation Not Confrontation (BCNC):
www.bcnc.org.uk

Dr Peter Breggin's: www.breggin.com

Recovery Road: www.recovery-road.org

Will Day's Benzo Recovery: www.willbenzo.com

Emotional Freedom Techniques (EFT)

Paula Kovacs, qualified EFT practitioner and benzo survivor
Website: www.benzorecovery.co.uk

Free EFT manual: *Introduction to EFT* by Gary Craig can be
downloaded at www.emofree.com

Books offering non-pharmacological approaches to anxiety and insomnia:

Bassett, Lucinda. *From Panic to Power: Proven Techniques to Calm Your Anxieties, Conquer Your Fears, and Put You in Control of Your Life.* Collins Living, 1996

Benson, Herbert. *The Relaxation Response.* Harper Paperbacks, 2000

Bourne, Edmund. *The Anxiety & Phobia Workbook.* New Harbinger Publications, 2005

Burns, David MD. *Feeling Good: The New Mood Therapy Revised and Updated.* Harper, 1999

Fletcher, E. & Langley, M. *Free Yourself From Anxiety.* Oxford: How To Books, 2009

Jacobs, Greg.D. *Say Good Night to Insomnia: The Six-Week, Drug-Free Program Developed At Harvard Medical School.* New York: Holt Publishing, 1998

Luciani, Joseph J. *Self-Coaching: The Powerful Program to Beat Anxiety and Depression, 2nd Edition, Completely Revised.* Wiley, 2006

Weekes, Claire. *Hope and Help For Your Nerves.* Signet, 1990

Relaxation Aids

Halpern, Steven. *Sleep Soundly.* Inner Peace Music, 1996

Harrold, Glen. *A Guided Meditation for Relaxation, Well Being and Healing.* Diviniti Publishing, 2002

Harrold, Glen. *Deep Sleep Every Night.* Diviniti Publishing, 2002

McManus, Carolyn PT, MA, MS. *Progressive Relaxation & Autogenic Training, 2003*

Naparstek, Belleruth. *A Meditation for Relaxation & Wellness.* Image Paths, 2002

Naparstek, Belleruth. *Health Journeys Guided Meditations For Help With Panic Attacks.* Health Journeys, 2007

Shapiro, Roberta. *The Calming Collection - Sleep Solutions, Guided meditation for restful sleep.* Sleep Solutions, 2006

Thompson, Jeffery DC. *Delta Sleep System.* The Relaxation Company, 1999

Suicide Helplines

Samaritans, UK: 08457 90 90 90
Website: www.samaritans.org

Samaritans, Republic of Ireland: 1850 60 90 90
Website: www.samaritans.org

Canada Suicide and Crisis Hotlines:
http://suicidehotlines.com/canada.html

National Suicide Prevention Lifeline,
USA: 1-800-273-TALK or 1-800-273-8255
Website: www.suicidepreventionlifeline.org

Sane Australia: 1-800-18-SANE or 1-800-18-7263
Website: www.sane.org

Worldwide helpline numbers: www.befrienders.org

Appendix 2
List of Common
Benzodiazepines

Generic Name	Brand Name
alprazolam	Xanax
bromazepam	Lexotan, Lexomil
chlordiazepoxide	Librium
clobazam	Frisium
clonazepam	Klonopin, Rivotril
clorazepate	Tranxene
diazepam	Valium, Ducene
flunitrazepam	Rohypnol
flurazepam	Dalmane
lorazepam	Ativan
nitrazepam	Mogadon
nordazepam	Nordaz, Calmday
oxazepam	Serax, Serepax, Serenid
temazepam	Restoril, Euhypnos, Normison
triazolam	Halcion

These 'Z' drugs are not benzodiazepines but have similar effects:

zaleplon	Sonata
zolpidem	Ambien, Stilnoct
zopiclone	Zimovane, Imovane
eszopiclone	Lunesta

Appendix 3
Equivalence Table

(Adapted from the *Ashton Manual* with the kind permission of Professor C. Heather Ashton.)

Benzodiazepine	Half-life (hrs) [active metabolite]	Approximate Equivalent Oral dosages mg
alprazolam (Xanax)	6-12	0.5
bromazepam (Lexotan, Lexomil)	10-20	5-6
chlordiazepoxide (Librium)	5-30 [36-200]	25
clobazam (Frisium)	12-60	20
clonazepam (Klonopin, Rivotril)	18-50	0.5
clorazepate (Tranxene)	[36-200]	15
diazepam (Valium)	20-100 [36-200]	10
flunitrazepam (Rohypnol)	18-26	1
flurazepam (Dalmane)	[40-250]	15-30
lorazepam (Ativan)	10-20	1
nitrazepam (Mogadon)	15-38	10
nordazepam (Nordaz, Calmday)	36-200	10
oxazepam (Serax, Serepax, Serenid)	4-15	20
temazepam (Restoril, Normison, Euhypnos)	8-22	20
triazolam (Halcion)	2	0.5

'Z' Drugs Equivalence

Z Drug	Half-life (hrs)	Approximate Equivalent Oral dosages mg
zaleplon (Sonata)	2	20
zolpidem (Ambien, Stilnoct)	2	20
zopiclone (Zimovane, Imovane)	5-6	15
eszopiclone (Lunesta)	6 (9 in elderly)	3

The information contained within this Appendix is based on clinical experience which was used to produce the *Ashton Manual*. The drug's half-life is the time taken for the blood concentration level to fall by fifty percent after a single dose. This is important to note when switching from one benzodiazepine to another. For example, if you plan on tapering using diazepam and your current dosage is 1.5 mg clonazepam daily, since 0.5 mg clonazepam is equivalent to 10 mg diazepam, you are taking the equivalent of 30 mg diazepam. The half-life of the active products of the drug or active metabolite, shown in square brackets, varies according to individual.

Appendix 4
Tapering Schedule Example

This is adapted from the *Ashton Manual's* Schedules 5 and 3 with kind permission. It is shown here as an example only and so the duration of each stage of reduction has been removed. If you are planning to taper, please consult your doctor or other healthcare provider to discuss and arrange your schedule.

Phase 1

Duration	Morning	Midday	Evening	Diazepam Equiv.
Starting dose	clonazepam 0.5 mg	clonazepam 0.5 mg	clonazepam 0.5mg	30 mg
	clonazepam 0.5 mg	clonazepam 0.5 mg	clonazepam 0.25 mg diazepam 5mg	30 mg
	clonazepam 0.5 mg	clonazepam 0.5 mg	STOP CLONAZEPAM diazepam 10 mg	30 mg
	clonazepam 0.25 mg diazepam 5mg	clonazepam 0.5 mg	diazepam 10 mg	30 mg
	clonazepam 0.25 mg diazepam 5mg	clonazepam 0.25 mg diazepam 5mg	diazepam 10 mg	30 mg
	STOP CLONAZEPAM diazepam 10 mg	clonazepam 0.25 mg diazepam 5 mg	diazepam 10 mg	30 mg
	diazepam 10 mg	STOP CLONAZEPAM	diazepam 10 mg	28 mg

Tapering Schedule (cont'd)

Phase 2

Duration	Morning	Midday	Evening	Diazepam Equiv.
	diazepam 10 mg	diazepam 6 mg	diazepam 10 mg	26 mg
	diazepam 10 mg	diazepam 4 mg	diazepam 10 mg	24 mg
	diazepam 10 mg	diazepam 2 mg	diazepam 10 mg	22 mg
	diazepam 10 mg	STOP DIAZEPAM	diazepam 10 mg	20 mg
	diazepam 8 mg	---	diazepam 10 mg	18 mg
	diazepam 6 mg	---	diazepam 10 mg	16 mg
	diazepam 4 mg	---	diazepam 10 mg	14 mg
	diazepam 2 mg	---	diazepam 10 mg	12 mg
	STOP DIAZEPAM	---	diazepam 10 mg	10 mg

Phase 3

Duration	Morning	Midday	Evening	Diazepam Equiv.
	---	---	diazepam 9 mg	9 mg
	---	---	diazepam 8 mg	8 mg
	---	---	diazepam 7 mg	7 mg
	---	---	diazepam 6 mg	6 mg
	---	---	diazepam 5 mg	5 mg
	---	---	diazepam 4 mg	4 mg
	---	---	diazepam 3 mg	3 mg
	---	---	diazepam 2 mg	2 mg
	---	---	diazepam 1 mg	1 mg
	---	---	STOP DIAZE-PAM	---

Appendix 5
Symptoms A to Z

A to Z List of Symptoms

Note: This list includes verbatim descriptions from Website users and is intended to be used as a reference only. The withdrawal experience is unique and you may end up *not* having any of these symptoms. If you do, they may be mild and last for a very short period. If you have already started tapering and are experiencing symptoms, please refer to only those that apply. **It is advisable to *not* read this prior to tapering.**

A

Abdominal cramps: cramping and pain in the abdomen, sometimes moving to different areas

Achiness: dull aches and pains all over the body

Agitation: restless, feeling a need to move around, 'antsy' feeling

Agoraphobia: fear of going out, fear of open spaces, fear of having panic attacks in unfamiliar places, often confined to home

Anger/Rage: often unexplained, tantrums, loss of temper with no apparent cause

Anxiety: adrenaline rushes, panic attacks, overbreathing, palpitations often including agoraphobia

Apathy: lack of motivation, lack of interest in self or others, emotionally flat, socially withdrawn, flatness

Appetite changes: loss, gain leading to increase or decrease in weight

B

Back pain: lower, mid, upper, coccyx

Balance problems/Dizziness: feeling unsteady on feet, room 'spinning' even when sitting or lying, feeling drunk

Benzo belly: distension, bloat, pot belly, abnormally large, looking 'pregnant'

Bloating/Water retention: oedema, swollen feet, swollen hands, eyelids, looking puffy

Blurred vision: everything appears blurred, problems reading and seeing generally

Body temperature: fluctuations

Brain fog: feeling as if observing through a cloud, reduced clarity

Brain motion: feeling of the brain moving inside head

Bruxism/Teeth grinding: occurs during sleep (often associated with tolerance or as a side effect while still on drug)

Burning pain/Sensations: on any part of body, often the shoulders, back, hands and feet

C

Concentration loss: inability to focus attention and/or acquire new information

Confusion: simple tasks are difficult, unable to decipher directions or follow simple instructions

Creaking joints: creaking with movement, 'cracking' sound in neck, arms, back, hips

Crawling sensation on skin: distorted perception - feeling as if insects are crawling all over (usually during acute withdrawal)

Crying spells: feeling weepy at times without being able to identify a specific trigger, inability to stop crying

D

Depersonalisation: altered perception, dissociated feelings, detached from self, feeling like alien in own body, disconnected

Depressive mood: low, heavy mood, flat affect, unmotivated, feeling of hopelessness

Derealisation: altered perception, dissociated feelings, feeling of being distant, cut off, being in a dream-like state, surreal

Dizziness/Balance problems: unsteady on feet, feeling as if drunk, room 'spinning' even when sitting or lying

Dreams: vivid, recurring, themed, nightmares with disturbing images

Dry mouth: mouth dry and feeling as if no saliva

E

Electric shock sensations/Zaps: feeling as if shocked, shocks running through body (any part including ears)

Emotional blunting or anaesthesia: inability to feel emotions whether positive or negative, not connected to authentic feelings

Exhaustion: extreme weakness, feeling totally without energy as if just completed a marathon, 'bone tired'

Extreme thirst: insatiable urge to keep drinking

Eyes: sore, dry, red, tired, blurred vision, double vision, floaters, glazed, glassy appearance

F

Face pain: face hurts all the time

Facial numbness: face numb/tingling, forehead numb, no feeling in one side of face, no feeling in both sides of face

False sensations of moving (perception distortion): feel as if body is moving or chair or bed

Fatigue/Lethargy: extreme tiredness, listlessness, lacking in energy

Fear (organic)/Impending doom: fear surpassing natural anxiety/concerns re withdrawal, not identifiable with a thought or feeling, feels inauthentic but overwhelming, scared that something 'terrible' is about to happen, intense fear of dying

Fits: epileptic like movements (rare, can be caused by cold turkeying)

Flu-like symptoms: feel as if getting flu with aches, joint/muscle pain, feverish, stuffy nose

G

Gastrointestinal disturbances/Stomach problems: Vomiting, diarrhoea, constipation, nausea, reflux, oesophageal spasms, feeling of choking, distension, stomach cramps

Glassy eyes: eyes look like those of a street drug addict's, glazed and shiny

H

Hair: change in texture, hair loss, breakage

Hallucinations: hypnagogic hallucinations or brief events when falling asleep, usually visual, tactile, sensual or auditory

Headaches/Tight band around head: feeling as if an imaginary band around head is constantly being tightened, throbbing pain in head, migraine-like headaches, pain in temples

Hearing hypersensitivity/Hyperacusis: exaggerated sound, cutlery, crockery, environmental sounds 'nerve-shatteringly loud', people sound as if they are shouting

Heart: palpitations, irregular beats, thumping, beating loudly, feels as if jumping out of chest cavity

Heaviness: part of the body, especially limbs, feel extremely heavy, body feels like 'lead'

Hormonal imbalances: including non-menopausal hot flashes, severe pre-menstrual tension

I

Inner trembling/Shaking/Vibrating (perception distortion): feeling of body trembling or vibrating 'on the inside'

Insomnia/Sleep disturbances: nights at a time without sleep, few hours sleep per night, waking up throughout the night, unable to go back to sleep

Intrusive memories: unwanted and persistent memory sometimes of traumatic events

Irritability: very low tolerance levels, easily irritated

J

Jelly legs: legs feel weak and rubbery as if about to give way

Joint/Muscle pain: joints hurt, joints feel arthritic and muscles hurt, muscles feel as if performed rigorous exercise

Jumpiness: on edge, startled by sounds or people, extremely nervous

L

Lethargy/Fatigue: extreme tiredness, listlessness, lacking in energy, unable to even sit up

Libido loss: loss of interest in sexual intercourse, inability to become aroused

Light hypersensitivity: everything seems intensely and unbearably bright, feeling the need to wear sun glasses even inside, unable to look at computer screen

M

Memory impairment: short-term memory loss, 'gaps in memory' where unable to recall specific events, memory lapses (side effect of drug as well as symptom)

Menstrual irregularity and dysmenorrhea: cycle changes and becomes irregular, painful periods

Metallic tastes: mouth has a metallic taste, gustatory distortion

Mood swings: extreme and rapid changes in moods, one minute feeling optimistic then very low, feeling 'bipolar', feeling manic then depressed

Moving sensations: false perceptions of body moving

Muscle twitches/Jerks/Spasms: involuntary movements - myoclonic jerks, tics, twitches and spasms in different areas of body including extremities

Muscle/Joint pain: joints feel arthritic and muscles stiff and hurting, muscles feel as if performed rigorous exercise

Muscular rigidity: muscles all over feel extremely stiff, inability to move agilely

N

Nail discolouration and splitting: nails change colour, nails yellow, look jaundiced, nails grey, weak and splitting

Nausea: feeling of wanting to throw up all the time, feeling of being seasick

Nightmares: vivid, unpleasant sometimes terrifying dreams

Numbness/Tingling: like paraesthesia, fingers, hand, face, sometimes entire body

O

Obsessive thoughts: repetitive, unwanted thoughts

Oedema/Water retention: fluid in body tissues, swollen feet, puffiness

Oesophageal problems: oesophageal spasms, reflux

Overbreathing: breathing faster and deeper than necessary, hyperventilating

P

Pain: different parts or all of body stiff and hurting

Palpitations: heart races, beats wildly, thumps, feels like jumping out of chest

Panic attacks: adrenaline rushes, feel as if dying, feeling unable to breathe, feel as if choking

Paranoid thoughts: unfounded, suspicious thoughts, feel threatened, feel persecuted

Perception Distortion:

Speech is distorted, unable to follow a conversation, time delay or inability to reconcile words being uttered with movement of mouth

False sensations of moving e.g. feeling as though falling through bed, chair or as if part of body is moving away

Visual (seeing 'things') e.g. flashing lights, inanimate objects appear to be moving, people appear flat, one-dimensional and paper-like, buildings leaning, undulating floors (wavelike movement)

Gustatory distortion, metallic taste in mouth

Tactile distortion, feeling of insects crawling on skin

Profuse sweating/Perspiring: rivulets of perspiration, bathed in perspiration but not feeling hot, sweating all the time even in air-conditioning, often during acute withdrawal

R

Rage/Anger: feeling violent, surge of anger, argumentative 'out of the blue', feeling urge to 'lash out'

Reading/Comprehension problems: inability to read, focus or understand even simple instruction

Repetitive/Obsessive thoughts: thoughts persist and interrupt cognition, can't stop unwanted thoughts going over and over in mind

Restless legs: sensation in legs, overwhelming urge to move legs when lying down, leg jerks while sleeping

S

Sexual dysfunction: loss of libido, erectile dysfunction, loss of interest in sexual intercourse

Shaking/Tremors: uncontrollable shaking and tremors, hands shake, part of body or whole body trembles

Skin problems: rashes, acne, itching, burning, stripping and other problems on different areas of skin

Sleep disturbance/Insomnia: nights at a time without sleep, few hours sleep per night, waking up throughout the night, unable to go back to sleep

Soft tissue pain: thighs and other fleshy areas of body hurt

Stomach problems/Gastrointestinal problems: vomiting, diarrhoea, nausea, reflux, oesophageal spasms, feeling of choking, distension, stomach cramps

Sweats/Chills: one minute perspiring profusely then freezing/shaking, hot flashes as if menopausal then shaking, hot then chills as if one has ague

Sweating: profuse sweating regardless of temperature, body washed in perspiration, clothes wet

T

Temperature: fluctuations in body temperature

Throat: sore, tight, choking sensation, spasming

Thoughts: repetitive, unwanted, obsessive, suicidal

Tinnitus: constant or intermittent ringing in the ears, high-pitched noise in ears

Tiredness: exhausted, void of energy

Tooth/Gum/Mouth pain: nerves in teeth hurt, gum hurts, all teeth in mouth hurt

Touch hypersensitivity: extreme sensitivity to touch

Tremors/Shaking: uncontrollable shaking and tremors, hands shake, part of body or whole body trembles

Twitching/Tics: muscles in different areas of body twitch, involuntary movements, vocal tics

U

Uncontrollable crying: unable to stop crying (for no apparent reason)

Urinary problems: frequency, urinary tract infections, partial or complete incontinence, bladder hypersensitivity, dysuria

V

Vision blurred or double: everything appears blurred, problems reading, seeing 'double'

Visual perception distortion: seeing 'things', inanimate objects appear to be moving, people and objects appear flat, one-dimensional and paper-like

W

Water retention/Oedema: fluid in body tissues, swollen feet, puffiness

Weakness: feel drained of energy, almost unable to move or even sit up

Weepiness: spontaneous crying spells without being able to identify a specific trigger

Weight issues: unexplained fluctuations in weight, inability to gain weight, inability to lose weight, benzo belly

Z

Zaps: electric shock sensations, feeling as if shocked, shocks running through body (any part including ears)

Bibliography

Ashton, C. Heather, 2002. *Benzodiazepines: How They Work and How to Withdraw* [online] available at www.benzo.org.uk [accessed June 26, 2006].

Boutenko, Victoria, 2005. *Green For Life*. Oregon: Raw Family Publishing.

British National Formulary 49, 2005. London: British Medical Association & Royal Pharmaceutical Society of Great Britain.

Diagnostic and Statistical Manual of Mental Disorders DSM-IV-TR (Text Revision), 2004. Washington DC: American Psychiatric Publishing, Inc.

Foster, H., 2004. *Easy G I Diet: Using the Glycaemic Index to Lose Weight and Gain Energy*. London: Octopus Publishing.

Freeman, D. & Garety, P.A. (2004) *Paranoia: The Psychology of Persecutory Delusions*. Hove: Psychology Press.

Greenblatt D.J., Shader R.I., Divoll M., Harmatz J.S. (1981). Benzodiazepines: a summary of pharmacokinetic properties. *British Journal of Clinical Pharmacology*. 11 (1), pp 11S–16S. Available at http://www.ncbi.nlm.nih.gov/pubmed/6133528 [accessed January 11, 2009].

Hay, Louise L, 2004. *Heal Your Body*. 4th ed. Carlsbad, CA: Hay House Publishing.

Hay, Louise L., 1999. *You Can Heal Your Life*. Carlsbad, CA: Hay House Publishing.

Jongsma E. & Peterson L., 2003. *Complete Adult Psychotherapy Treatment Planner*. New Jersey: John Wiley & Sons.

Lader M., Tylee A., Donoghue J., (2009).Withdrawing benzodiazepines in primary care. *CNS Drugs* 23 (1), pp.19–34.

Miller, W. R. & Rollnick, S., 2002. *Motivational Interviewing*. NY: Guildford Press.

Rang, H.P., Dale, M.M. & Ritter, J.M., 1999. *Pharmacology*. 4th ed. Edinburgh: Churchill Livingstone.

Shawshank Redemption, 1994. [Film] Directed by Frank Durabont. USA: Castle Rock Entertainment.

Sommer-Flanagan J. & R., *Clinical Interviewing*. 3rd ed. NJ: Wiley & Sons.

WHO Expert Committee on Addiction-Producing Drugs. *Thirteenth report of the WHO Expert Committee*. Geneva, World Health Organization, 1964 (WHO Technical Report Series, No.273).

Weekes, Claire, 1977. *Self-Help For Your Nerves*. London: Thorsons.

Wisneski, L. A., & Anderson, L. (2004) *The Scientific Basis of Integrative Medicine*. Boca Raton FL: CRC Press.

Woods M.G., Williams D.C., 1996. Multiple forms and locations for the peripheral-type benzodiazepine receptor. *Biochemical Pharmacology*. 52(12), pp.1805–1814.

Index

S

T

CPSIA information can be obtained at www.ICGtesting.com
230288LV00002B/131/P